CORRESPONDENCES *of the* BIBLE

T0350734

Three volumes in this series by John Worcester

Correspondences of the Bible: The Animals

Correspondences of the Bible: The Plants

Correspondences of the Bible: The Human Body

CORRESPONDENCES *of the* BIBLE

The Plants

The Minerals

and The Atmospheres

John Worcester

Swedenborg Foundation Press
West Chester, Pennsylvania

First edition published in 1888
by the Massachusetts New-Church Union, Boston
Reprinted in 1930 by the Massachusetts
New-Church Union, Boston
Reprinted in 2009 by the Swedenborg Foundation,
West Chester, Pennsylvania

Correspondences of the Bible by John Worcester
The Animals ISBN 978–0–87785–112–7
The Plants ISBN 978–0–87785–113–4
The Human Body ISBN 978–0–87785–114–1
Three-volume set ISBN 978–0–87785–111–0

Scanned and edited by Everett Scholfield
Edited by Lee Woofenden, with assistance from the Information
Management Support Unit of the General Convention
Additional editing, notes, and index by Morgan Beard
Designed and typeset by Karen Connor

Printed in the United States of America

For more information:
Swedenborg Foundation Press
320 North Church Street • West Chester, PA 19380
www.swedenborg.com

Contents

Contents

Contents

Contents

About This Book

Correspondences refer to the spiritual meaning behind everyday objects or ideas. For example, the heat and light of the sun correspond to God's love and wisdom, so heat and love and light and wisdom are correspondences. Throughout this book, Worcester gives examples of how specific animals represent certain spiritual principles, and you can read more in the companion volumes *The Animals* and *The Human Body*. These correspondences reflect the inner meaning of the Bible.

John Worcester originally wrote *The Plants* in 1888 as an aid to studying correspondences as described in the writings of Emanuel Swedenborg (1688–1772).

Emanuel Swedenborg was a Swedish scientist, inventor, and mystic who spent his life investigating the mysteries of the soul. Born in Stockholm to a staunchly Lutheran family, he graduated from the University of Uppsala and then traveled to England, Holland, France, and Germany to study the leading scientists of the time. He gained favor with Sweden's King Charles XII, who gave him a position overseeing the Swedish mining industry. Later, he was granted a seat on the Swedish House of Nobles by Charles XII's successor, Queen Ulrika Eleonora.

Between 1743 and 1745, a lifetime of religious study culminated in personal contact with the spiritual realms. He wrote a steady stream of books describing his experiences traveling in spirit form through heaven and hell, his conversations with angels and demons, and the inner meaning of the Bible as revealed to him through the Lord.

Because this volume was written for Swedenborgians, Swedenborg's books are cited without bibliographic information, and occasionally the author uses terms which are specific to Swedenborgian studies. Worcester's original footnotes are preserved in the text, but in some places a footnote has been added with an asterisk (*) to explain terms which may be unfamiliar to non-Swedenborgians. A full list of Emanuel Swedenborg's spiritual books is included in the back of this volume to aid those who would like to do more research.

Correspondences *of the* Bible

The Correspondence of Plants

THE CORRESPONDENCE OF PLANTS WITH ELEMENTS OF humanity is less evident than that of animals; for the activity and demonstrativeness of animals force upon us a recognition of their likeness to ourselves, and call out our sympathy with the affections and passions which they exhibit. But plants, on the other hand, are stationary and passive; they seem less like living creatures, and, consequently, less like men. Yet there is a very real delight in the companionship and cultivation of plants of various kinds: the silent forests have power to excite human feeling in harmony with themselves; the daisies and violets typify to everyone's perception certain human attributes; the brilliant purples, crimsons, and scarlets of our cultivated flowers surely have some relation to the thrills of human feeling which quicken our hearts as we look at them; that "the Sower soweth the Word," is accepted as a perfect truth, without question of the correspondence it implies between seed grain and principles of human life; an institution for implanting such principles we call a "seminary"; and we give the name of "nurseries" alike to the ground in which young trees are growing, the neighborhoods in which new principles are cherished, and the rooms for tending little children. There can be no doubt of our recognition of a general relation between the plants around us and the principles, theories, and plans in our minds.

It is the teaching of the New Church* that this relation is that of full correspondence; that the same creative influence which, received by human minds, gives the power of knowing, of perceiving truth, and of developing principles of life to their natural fruit, received by suitable materials in the earth, manifests itself as plant life; and that the phenomena presented by this life in the vegetable kingdom represent perfectly, as to all the processes of growth as well as the varieties of form, the growths of intelligence and wisdom in the mind.

Speaking generally, animals are distinguished from plants by powers of locomotion, by sensitiveness, and by feeding upon vegetable substances. And there are corresponding general differences between affection and wisdom.

Affection is ever in motion, entering with sympathy into new states, and adapting itself to new circumstances; but definite forms of knowledge are based upon definite sets of facts, and there they remain. If transplanted to other dissimilar sets, they accommodate themselves with difficulty, though new plants of the same kinds might readily grow from seed. A love of being helpful, for instance, enters readily into entirely new situations, wherever help is needed; but definite knowledge of what is helpful must be based upon circumstances; a theory formed for one situation will rarely flourish in another; and the difficulty is the greater as the theory is more mature, and its details more fully developed.

Affection, again, is sensitive, and conscious of pleasure or pain; knowledge in itself, and separated from the affections which enjoy it, is sensible neither of growth nor of

---

* Also known as the Church of the New Jerusalem, this is the church based on the teachings of Emanuel Swedenborg.

mutilation. There is an affection for thinking, which is delighted with the act of intelligent perception, and is pained by obscurity. But a theory, a plan, or knowledge of any kind, in the mind, has no sense of pleasure or of pain; though its development may give a very keen enjoyment to the affections which meditate upon it, either in pride or in charity or in simple love for truth.

The third general distinction between plants and animals is that plants live upon inorganic materials from the earth and the air, while animals need to have these materials organized for them by plants. The mental correlative of this fact is that wisdom grows by the application of general truth to particular circumstances; but that affection is not expanded by general, abstract truth, until this is embodied in definite knowledge of states or forms of life which are lovely. General truths concerning the duty of uprightness and usefulness have a moderating and purifying effect upon the affections, but have no power to enlarge them; they present no definite object of interest and satisfaction. But from these truths, with some acquaintance with present circumstances and opportunities, definite social theories and plans for useful work may grow up, which furnish materials for meditation and new activity and enlarged enjoyment to the affections.

These distinctions between animals and plants are clearly defined and easily recognized in the higher types of the two kingdoms; but the simplest living organisms consist merely of minute specks of protoplasm, called monads, endowed with powers of motion, of nourishment, and of reproduction, with regard to some of which it seems impossible to determine whether they are animals or plants. There is a corresponding meeting of mental growths on the lowest plane of spiritual life—the plane of sensation. Do an infant's first impressions belong to the domain of understanding or of affection? Are his first intentional sounds expressive of thought or of feeling? Is it possible to distinguish in these first productions of his mind thought from feeling? This seems to be common ground.

Again, in speaking of affection and wisdom as entirely distinct and in contrast with each other, we are using the terms in a manner which needs some qualification; for, wisdom does not grow from facts and abstract truth without some desire and effort to be wise, by which the abstract truth is seized and applied and organized. And this desire to be wise is itself an affection which is the formative life of the wisdom. But it is affection operating in a purely intellectual way, giving rise to purely intellectual developments. The same affection which produces the intellectual growths also loves them when produced—produces them for the sake of enjoying them. Thus, it is not too much to say that one and the same affection operating in our faculty for becoming wise produces spiritual plants; and, exhibited in its proper nature as a living affection, produces also those enjoyments in the fruits of wisdom which are spiritual animals.

This is curiously illustrated by Swedenborg from his experience in the spiritual world. He says:

> The origin of animals, which also is their soul, is a spiritual affection, such as belongs to man in his natural degree. . . . That plants also have the same origin is evident, especially from the plants in the heavens, as that they appear there according to the affections of the angels, and also represent those

affections, insomuch that in them as in their types, the angels see and know their own affections, as to their nature and quality.... The only difference is that the affections appear formed into animals by the spiritual life in its middle principles, and into plants in its lowest, which are the earths there; for the spiritual life from which they exist, in middle principles, is alive, but not so in the lowest, in which the spiritual influence retains no more of life than is sufficient to produce the likeness of it.... That the plant soul is from the same origin as the soul of the beasts of the earth, of the birds of the heaven, and of the fishes of the sea, does not appear at first view, by reason that the one lives and the other does not; but still it is manifestly evident from the animals and plants seen in heaven, and also from those seen in hell. In the heavens there appear beautiful animals and beautiful plants; but in the hells noxious animals and also similar plants; and angels and spirits are known and their qualities distinguished by the appearance of the animals, and likewise of the plants; there is a full correspondence [of both] with their affections, and so much so that an animal can be changed into a correlative plant, and a plant into a correlative animal. (*Apocalypse Explained* §1212)

Plants represent affections in the effort to be wise, and to gather the elements of knowledge which in themselves are dead, and to arrange them in their relations to life and duty so that they may give enjoyment and support to the living affections; animals represent the affections themselves in their activity and enjoyment. Plants express the loveliness of wisdom and the goodness of the works of wisdom, produced by and living from affection; animals show forth the warm life of the affection, with its delight in wisdom and in the fruits of wisdom.

The Fruit Trees

The Olive

THE TREE WHICH, FROM THE IMPORTANCE OF ITS BENE-
fits and the honor paid to it in ancient times, appears to
represent in fullest measure the sacred influence of the
Tree of Life, is the Olive. It is a modest tree, of abounding
fruitfulness, with graceful, yielding twigs, willow-shaped
evergreen leaves, of dark olive tint above and silvery
beneath, and a trunk which, as it grows old, allows its useless inner wood to decay away, preserving only the outer
layers still serviceable to the fruit, which split up into a
picturesque group of distinct, irregular stems.

Its flowers are small, white, four-lobed, very plentiful,
giving place, as the season advances, to a generous abundance of olives. The trees readily grow from seeds, but
they need grafting; for the fruit of the wild olive is small
and dry. An olive tree begins to bear at about twelve years
of age, but does not attain maturity until it has lived forty
years. After that, if carefully tended, it can be depended
upon for an annual yield of ten to fifteen gallons of oil for
an indefinite period. No one knows how long it may live;
but there are old trees in the neighborhood of Jerusalem
believed to have grown from the stumps left by Titus
when he destroyed the city in the year seventy.

Some of the olives are pickled, and constitute an important article of food in the countries where they grow; but

most are pressed in the mill for their oil. The oil is pure nourishment, and is used freely in its native land as we use butter. It is also burned in lamps for its rich warm light, is made into soap, and is used everywhere to soothe and soften bruises and wounds, and to relieve the friction of delicate machinery.

These soothing, healing, cheering, nourishing properties indicate, as the spiritual correlative of olive oil, a knowledge of some merciful goodness. Only this would at once give so much support and nourishment to the mind, heal its wounds and bruises, relieve social friction and chafing, and furnish a standard of goodness by which, as in clear light, spiritual things can be seen truly and in their just relations.

But, while a knowledge of some kindly affection is surely represented by oil, there are many sorts and degrees of kindness which would answer the purpose more or less perfectly. Yet there are some things which are true of the oil of olives which can be said of no other oil; and there is a noble love which is similarly distinguished from every other kindly love. It is the purest and sweetest of all the oils which answer these useful purposes; and it was appointed, in the Divinely selected ceremonial of the Jews, as the means of consecration of priests and kings, and of all the buildings and furniture used in the service of the Lord. The only love of which corresponding spiritual things can be said with truth, is the merciful love of the Lord received consciously as from Him by men. The goodness which men in penitent states feel in their hearts when they humble them before the Lord, is mercy itself; it is absolutely unselfish love. It is known by no man so long as he thinks he is good of himself, and lives from his own impulses, guided by his own reason; but when he is fully conscious of his natural worthlessness and opens his heart to the Lord, a new love enters, and he begins to know how good the Lord is. The knowledge of the goodness of God which men have before they know the Lord as their God and their Savior is like the small dry berries of the wild olive (*True Christian Religion* §537). But the knowledge they have after they know and acknowledge Him is like generous olives full of oil.

With such knowledge of the goodness of the Lord, kings and priests ought to be consecrated; for their business is to rule over natural and spiritual affairs from the Divine love of doing good to men. The Lord's own Humanity was called "the Messiah"; that is, "the Anointed," because He came to do upon the earth the works of the Divine Love. Such oil, also, is the "oil of joy" and the "oil of gladness" by which the faces of those who know and love the Lord are made to shine.

All the spiritual uses which correspond to the natural uses of oil, such knowledge of the Divine goodness per - forms preeminently well. Above all other knowledge it flames with warm light, showing all things as the Lord's own goodness sees them. It brings healing and strength and support to the deep places of the spirit. It is a knowledge of pure mercy, and gives patient charity amid social conflicts. It also cleanses the soul from stains which, like resin and fat, resist the water of purification; for, by the revelation of the Lord's generous goodness, it makes us ashamed of selfish indulgences to which we cling though we know they are wrong, and loosens their hold upon us.

The tree upon which this excellent fruit is borne may be named from the fruit, *the tree of knowledge of the Lord's goodness*. Its seed is the confession that the Lord is good, encased in a stony shell from the truth that "none is good but One: God."

Planted in the soil of a good heart, this seed sends down its roots among the facts of creation, of human history, and of the Lord's Providence, seeking a solid foundation for its knowledge. Its leaves it raises into the air and sunshine, in the perennial desire to perceive the goodness of the Lord, and to lay up actual experiences of it. The materials gathered by the leaves are those which constitute the knowledge of the Lord's goodness which olive oil represents; the leaves are therefore the faculty of feeling or perceiving that goodness among the various influences of life.

But it is one thing to perceive intelligently the Lord's goodness in His works and His Providence, and quite another to feel His love for doing good as a living spring in us when opportunity to do good is offered. The gladness of this most delicate and living perception is represented by the plentiful yet modest blossoms of the tree, which are the beginning of fruitfulness.

The fruit of the natural tree is bitter when young, but in maturity is a sack of pure oil held firmly in its tissues, surrounding the single stony seed. Spiritually to mature the corresponding fruit is to bring into life the pure kindness perceived in the works of the Lord, and given from Him to His servants. They who are in the effort to live from the Lord know better than others the pride of heart which naturally prevents the proper reception of His love, and the chastening of self which is constantly needed to bring it forth in purity. Their fruit, while immature, is necessarily bitter, though when mature it is the Lord's own goodness. And every fruit contains a new assurance that the Lord, and the Lord alone, is good—an assurance alive with new desire to taste His goodness.

Of the fruit of the olive, we have a Divine example in Psalm 103—a Psalm which is full of perception and acknowledgment of the goodness of the Lord:

Bless Jehovah, O my soul;
And all that is within me, bless His holy name,
Bless Jehovah, O my soul,
And forget not all His benefits;
Who forgiveth all thine iniquities,
Who healeth all thy diseases;
Who redeemeth thy life from destruction,
Who crowneth thee with loving kindness
and tender mercies;
Who satisfieth thy mouth with good,
Thy youth is renewed like the eagle.

In the Mount of Olives our Lord was wont to rest after His days of labor in Jerusalem, because it represented His state of reception of the Father's Love, which comforted and sustained Him.

"An olive leaf plucked off"—a remnant of the life before the flood—was brought by the dove to Noah; which may be taken as a symbol of the perceptions of the Lord's goodness, traditionally handed down to the second Church* from the days of innocent openness to the Lord represented by Adam, and received not as a thing of perception, but of faith (*Arcana Coelestia* §879). Growing upon the tree, it is a perception; plucked off for another, it is a thing of faith.

Such perception of the Lord's mercy the second Church had not; but the Lord's love is a love of doing good, and when received by men it may be felt secondarily as a delight

---

* Swedenborg uses the term "church" not to refer to a particular Christian denomination or to a particular church building, but to a period in human history. He described five distinct ages, the second of which is the Ancient Church, which held sway from the Flood until the Ten Commandments were received by Moses.

in doing good to the neighbor. This secondary representation of the olive remained as a living thing in this
Church, and was cultivated by learning the ways of goodness and living in them. The Lord's love perceived as
mercy for us is called by Swedenborg "celestial good"; perceived as love for the neighbor it is called "spiritual good"
or "charity"; both are represented by the olive (*Arcana
Coelestia* §10261).

The knowledge of holy states, which has been preserved
in a Divine manner in our Sacred Scriptures, has come
down less perfectly, and still in forms full of interest, in
the myths and traditional customs of the Greeks and
Romans. In the prayers of the ancient Greeks, "in cases of
great distress, the suppliant would carry an olive branch,
or a rod with wool twined round it, throw himself on the
ground before the sacred image, and embrace its feet"
(Murray's *Manual of Mythology*, p. 16), which custom
seems to imply at some time a knowledge that a state of
dependence upon the Divine Mercy is expressed alike by
an olive branch and by lambs' clothing.

The Olympian Games were trials of skill—intellectual
and physical—held in honor of Zeus the supreme God, on
the plain of Olympia. The prize of excellence was simply a
wreath of olive (p. 17); as if in confession that a knowledge
of the goodness of God is the chief of human wisdom.

Apparently for the same reason, it is related of Pallas
Athene (cálled Minerva by the Romans), the goddess of
wisdom, that she caused the first olive tree to grow from
the bare rock of the Acropolis; and for this greatest of possible benefits to mankind she received the sovereignty of
the land (p. 58). The prize of the games in her honor, at
the festival called *Panathenæa*, "was a large painted earth-
enware vase filled with pure olive oil, the product of the
tree sacred to Athene" (p. 113). One could hardly express

more plainly the truth that a knowledge of the Divine Goodness is the noblest wisdom.

The Vine

THE VINE RANKS WITH FRUIT TREES IN EVERY RESPECT but this—that it clings to other upright objects for support. It sends out branches in profusion; but they can only run on the ground, lifting their heads a little, and requiring for the perfection of their fruit a tree or wall by which they may lift themselves into the air. When cut back continually, so that the branches are very small in proportion to the woody stem, the vine may stand upright like a small weeping tree; in which form it is cultivated in many vineyards.

It puts forth from the axils of the leaves tendrils, which are modified branches, or bunches of grapes, by which it raises itself to its supports. When thus sustained it produces clusters of fruit, composed mostly of sweet, spirited juice, with four hard, bony seeds. So very generous is it of its fruitfulness that, if unwisely encouraged, a noble vine will exhaust itself in a single season and die. To ripen its fruit properly, it needs much pruning and much sunshine. The fruit, however, varies greatly in quality, according to the kind of the vine, sometimes being sour and astringent, sometimes exceedingly pleasant. The leaves of the vine are large, and are said to be much liked by sheep and cattle.

That the vine is perennial, like fruit trees, and bears useful fruits, shows that it corresponds to some enduring principle which produces good works. That it naturally twines about other objects, depending upon them, and maturing no good fruit unless it be supported in the air, indicates that the principle to which it corresponds is sympathetic and very susceptible of spiritual elevation, which, indeed, is necessary to the value of its works. Its tendrils represent an affection for drawing near to others, especially in elevated states; and they are in the place of branches, or bunches of grapes, because this affection is desirous of giving, not of taking away.

The fruits of the vine are scarcely more than sacks of sweet and spirited juice, containing four seeds. The juice is composed of water drawn up from the earth by the vine, exposed to air and sunshine in the leaves, and by combination with elements of the air and sunshine, which are absorbed by the leaves, transformed to nourishing, refreshing juice, which is deposited in the grapes.

This is the use of the vine—to draw water from the earth and transform it into wine. It represents an affection which transforms the literal precepts of the Word into pleasant truth of spiritual life. It is an affection for teaching the Lord's commandments as truth of heavenly life as well as of natural, as the ways of interior happiness as well as of duty. It draws water of life from the letter of the Word, considers it in its application to states of thought and feeling, and, in the light and warmth of the Love that gave it, perceives its necessity to good, happy life, and thus fills it with affection and wisdom.

The spiritual Olive brings a knowledge of the Lord's goodness into human life; and the vine brings the kindness and pleasantness of His wisdom. But it is the pleasantness of wisdom relating to spiritual life, not to worldly and social advantages; the rich fruit is not perfected upon the ground.

In regard to the growth of spiritual vines, it may be said that when men come to a knowledge of spiritual truth they are at first only too eager to study it and talk about it with everybody. Some find delight in following out spiritual study in every direction, and are like vines that run to leaves and branches. Some are exceedingly zealous to enlighten and improve the world, and exhaust themselves in unwise fruitfulness. Experience comes as a pruner to direct the study wisely, and to secure moderation of incipient fruitfulness. Fortunate if it comes before the time of rank confusion, or of utter discouragement.

Patiently to think out the principles of spiritual life, as applied to one's home or to the community, with a perception of the Lord's blessing in the truth, is to mature the fruit of the vine; and it is manifest that the same effort which, chastened and wisely directed to improvement of life, will mature sweet and inspiriting wisdom; if allowed to generalize at random, may produce only immature and useless dogmatism; or, absorbed in unpractical speculations, may bring forth nothing but leaves. Even these may be serviceable to innocent natural states, though they are not helpful to spiritual life, as vine leaves are food for sheep and cattle, but not for man. There are also grapes which are not immature, but are essentially sour; and there are men who study the Bible and teach from it what they call the truth of Heaven, without any true knowledge of the Lord, or right reception of Him, and who therefore teach as truth of spiritual life what is distasteful and unwholesome.

The fruit of the olive relates to the Lord's goodness, or to mutual love from Him, and is, therefore, single, or grouped a few together. The fruit of the vine relates to the manifold duties of life, and hangs in clusters of many (*Apocalypse Explained* §918).

Its seeds are in two pairs, because its vital principles relate to the conjunction of goodness and truth, and of spiritual life and natural. They are hard and bony, because they are mostly composed of the unyielding truth that the words of the Lord are spirit and life, which their works are perpetually demonstrating with a delight which renews the desire to prove it again.

The Lord called Himself "the True Vine"; and at the marriage in Cana of Galilee He actually transformed water into wine, to represent the spiritual work which He was continually doing. He fulfilled the Law by living it Himself, and presenting it with deeper meaning and kind affection manifested in it. The Ten Blessings, and the remainder of the Sermon on the Mount, are the living water of the Ten Commandments applied to interior life and filled with charity.

The Commandment is, "Thou shalt not kill," which is rendered by the Vine of spiritual life. "Blessed are the merciful, for they shall obtain mercy." The Commandment says, "Thou shalt not commit adultery"; the Gospel, "Blessed are the pure in heart, for they shall see God." The Law enjoins love for the neighbor and hatred for the enemy; Jesus says, "Love your enemies, bless them that curse you, do good to them that hate you, and pray for them that despitefully use you and persecute you; that ye may be the children of your Father who is in Heaven."

The Commandments thus applied to the inner life, and filled with affection for the goodness which they teach, are spiritual wine. This is such wine as is represented by the wine of the Holy Supper, which, again, the Lord calls His "blood," because it is the thought of His own heart, which not only gives life, but is life to those who receive it.

They who love to think Christian truth from Him and to live it, the Lord calls His branches. Frequently throughout the Scriptures the Church is likened to a vine or a vineyard, as in the eightieth Psalm: "Thou hast brought a vine out of Egypt: Thou hast cast out the heathen and planted it"; and in Matthew 21:33: "There was a certain householder who planted a vineyard, and hedged it round about, and digged a wine press in it, and built a tower, and let it out to husbandmen, and went into a far country." Of Noah, also, who represents the second Church upon earth, it is said that he "planted a vineyard" (Genesis 9:20); because the characteristic of that Church was the study of spiritual truth such as is revealed by correspondences, and the enjoyment of the spiritual charity and beautiful living which such truth teaches. But it is added that Noah "drank of the wine and was drunken" (Genesis 5:21), which signifies that by correspondences and reasonings from natural things concerning spiritual, the Church fell into errors and became delirious (*Arcana Coelestia* §1072); as men do who use spiritual truth to exalt themselves, or for any other purpose than to increase their consciousness of dependence upon the Lord, and their love of doing His Commandments. The misuse of wine to produce drunkenness is frequently mentioned in the Word, and always with the signification of the abuse of spiritual truth to minister to one's pride or other selfishness. This is very evident in Isaiah: "Woe unto them that are wise in their own eyes, and prudent in their own sight. Woe unto them that are mighty to drink wine, and men of strength to mingle strong drink; who justify the wicked for reward, and take away the righteousness of the righteous from him" (Isaiah 5:21–23). The perverse application of spiritual truth, by which the Roman Catholic Church has granted indulgences and pardoned all manner of crimes to increase her own wealth and power, is meant by these words in the Apocalypse*: "The inhabitants of the earth have been made drunk with the wine of her fornication" (Revelation 17:2).

---

* The Book of Revelation.

Swedenborg speaks of an odor of wine which he perceived, and says, "I was informed that it was from those who from friendship and rightful love compliment one another, but so that there is truth in the compliments. The odor is with much variety, and is from the sphere of the beautiful in forms" (*Arcana Coelestia* §1517). No doubt there is a right use for wine, in great moderation, as a correspondence of and an aid to such friendly thought of others. The same flattery addressed to oneself, produces a silly complacency and self-display.

Swedenborg compares the purification of conjugial love* and its wisdom to the purification of alcoholic spirits, and adds "wisdom purified may be compared to alcohol, which is spirit most highly rectified" (*Conjugial Love* §145). On the other hand he says that the doctrine of justification by faith alone "has intoxicated the thoughts" of the clergy "like the spirit of wine which is called alcohol, so that, like the drunken, they have not seen this most essential thing of the church, that Jehovah God descended and assumed the Human" (*True Christian Religion* §98). The sugar, which is transformed into alcohol, has a correspondence with the natural pleasantness of thinking truth of spiritual wisdom; when transformed, it corresponds with a spiritual pleasantness, or assurance that the truth is the very truth of life. The process of fermentation seems to correspond with the freeing of the truth from that which is of self, which is in it from the process of thinking, and changing the natural pleasantness of it into a sense that it is not of self, but is of the truth of life. Asso-

---

* In Swedenborgian studies, the word conjugial (deliberately spelled with the extra i) refers to things belonging to marriage and the love married partners have for each other.

ciated with true wisdom, this assurance brings content; but associated with false doctrines it brings a fallacious security which is like drunkenness. Genuine truth from the Lord, teaching love to the Lord and the neighbor, with the assurance that it is the very truth of life, is the "wine that maketh glad the heart of man"—the good wine which the presence of the Lord produces for those who take part in the heavenly marriage of goodness with truth.

In describing his passage through the dark forest which protected the angels of the inmost heaven, Swedenborg says that his eyes were opened, and he saw olive trees entwined with vines, and his steps were led from olive to olive, till he reached the summit of the mountain (*Conjugial Love* §75). The olives are knowledge of the Lord's goodness; the vines are knowledge of the excellent kindness of His truth. Through states marked by the attainment of such knowledge lies the way to the angels nearest the Lord.

The Palm

OF THE APPEARANCE AND NATURAL HISTORY OF THE PALM tree we can have no better account than is contained in Mr. Grindon's admirable chapter (*Intellectual Repository*, August, 1873). He says:

> The palm is a living pillar, slender, cylindrical, and erect, and capable, in one species or another, of attaining the stature of sixty, eighty, one hundred, and even one hundred and ninety feet. Of lateral growth, such as would constitute umbrageousness,

like that of an oak or chestnut, there is none— not a single sideways shoot breaks the slim and shafted uniformity; the leaves, unique in their kind, measure many yards in length; they are as large, that is to say, as the entire branch of many an inferior tree of other formation; and, confined to the summit of the pillar, constitute a prodigious and evergreen crown, the principal leaves—such of them at least as are in the full vigor of existence—arching elegantly outwards and downwards. Because of these great dimensions, emulated only by the foliage of bananas and the arborescent ferns, they are called whenever mentioned in Scripture, not "leaves," but what they really seem to be, as when the people "took *branches* of palm trees and strewed them in the way." For the same reason, in the ancient poets, it is never the leaf, but always the "branch," of the palm that we read of. . . . Like those of most other evergreens, the leaves, individually, are long-lived. Of course they die in time; but the decay is often gradual, the long petiole preserving its foothold, though drooping, and remaining attached for a considerable period; and when it goes there is still usually left a fibrous and projecting stump, though sometimes only a scar. . . . No tree, not even the willow, is fonder of, or more dependent upon, water than the palm. Let the sunshine be ever so fervent, give water enough to the grateful root, and it sees not "when heat cometh"; flourishing so much the more gloriously under the twofold influence, though dying if moisture be withheld. Hence it is that the appearance of the particular kind of palm always intended in Scripture, the date palm, becomes, in the deserts where it grows spontaneously, an infallible indication of the presence of springs; and nowhere is the association more remarkable than in the northern part of the Sahara. Here the palm islands, or "oases," are so numerous as to constitute a vast archipelago; the district itself receiving the name of Beled-el-Jerid, or the "date country." The oases are not, as often supposed, islands of verdure that rise *above* the surrounding sand, but *depressions* in the sea—like expanse, in which moisture can be col - lected and retained, and where both animal life and vegetable can not only be supported, but sheltered from the storms—the latter an important element in the usefulness they subserve, and giving no slight enrichment to the familiar and expressive metaphor which makes the "oasis in the desert" another name for solace and refuge. The great charm of the oasis is that, however, which is found in the alliance of the palm, the emblem of victory, with water, the emblem, so constantly employed in Scripture, of Christian purity and Christian truth.

The flowers of the palm trees are fashioned much after the same plan as those of the lily, having all their parts in threes. Individually they make no show, and are often trifling and unattractive; but the abundance is so vast that, were all to result in fruit, scarcely any plants in nature could be esteemed more *fecund*. The many-branched clusters, often several feet in length, are developed from the very apex of the stem, sometimes standing erect, and constituting an immense thyrsus; more usually hanging down from among the bases of the leaf stalks. While young, the whole mass of the inflorescence is enclosed in a peculiar sheath, termed a "spathe," just as in England we may see the panicles of many grasses wrapped round before expansion by the uppermost green leaf.

The staminate and the pistillate flowers of the palm grow upon separate trees. To secure a crop of dates, therefore, the Arabs are in the habit of cutting the bunches of flowers from a stamen-bearing tree, and tying them among the clusters of pistillate flowers on another tree.

The date palm, the only species of the order made mention of in Scripture, is a tree of sixty to eighty feet in height, less graceful in appearance than some of the others, but in substantial usefulness excelled by none. No palm is in any way deleterious, and the variety of useful products obtained from the order in general has no parallel; the date palm stands, nevertheless, quite at the head, if only from the vast multitude of human beings it sup - plies with sustenance. But this is not all; the leaves are employed for various household purposes, and for fodder; and the very stones of the fruits, hard and worthless as they seem, when ground up with water, serve as food for horses and camels.

The tall, straight trunk of the palm, stretching up into the heaven, and expanding its great leaves at the top, is suggestive of some spiritual principle that looks directly to the Lord. The precise nature of this principle is indicated by the use that is made of palms in the Scriptures.

We read in John chapter 12 that the people "took branches of palm trees," and went forth to meet the Lord, and cried, "Hosanna; blessed is the King of Israel that cometh in the name of the Lord."

"Branches of palm trees" are, as has been shown, the large palm leaves. From the ancient times, when their meaning was known, came down the custom of giving palm leaves to conquerors as emblems of victory. Nike, the goddess of victory, was therefore represented by the Greeks as carrying a "palm branch" in her hand (Murray, p. 213).

The people carried them to the Lord, and went before Him waving them, to express the same feeling that found another utterance in their words, "Blessed be the King of Israel, that cometh in the name of the Lord." The palm leaves, therefore, here represent the acknowledgment of the Lord as King of Israel, coming in the name and with the power of Jehovah.

In the Apocalypse (chapter 7), it is said that "a great multitude stood before the throne and before the Lamb, clothed in white robes and palms in their hands; and cried with a loud voice, saying, 'Salvation to our God who sitteth upon the throne, and unto the Lamb.'" Here again, the meaning of the palms is explained by the spoken words which ascribe salvation to the Divinity and the Divine Humanity of the Lord.

Palm leaves in the hand are, then, acknowledgments of the Lord as King and Savior; and growing upon their native tree they are *perceptions* of the Divine saving power of the Lord. The tree from which such perceptions spring, and which in turn they increase and strengthen, is the *tree of belief in the Lord.*

This tree reaches up directly toward the Lord; with no branches, but bearing at its highest point these rational perceptions of His Divine attributes. It springs up in the desert of the natural mind in youth and early manhood when the passions are hot, wherever the cooling influence of the Divine truth of life from the Word is felt and cordially received. Such reception of cleansing truth, and experience of its use, prepares the mind for belief in the Lord as our Savior and King.

Therefore it was that as soon as the children of Israel crossed the Jordan, by which this spiritual cleansing was signified, they came to Jericho, "the city of palm trees"— the first city they entered of their Holy Land, and therefore representing the first state of good life from faith in the Lord.

On account of its situation, low in the Jordan valley, the climate of Jericho is tropical, well suited to the palm tree, which gives place to the fig and the olive as we climb the hills toward the interior of the land. And, in like manner, the principles represented by the palm flourish best with those who have more zeal than wisdom; and whose works also are, in their manner of initiation, imaged by the fertilization of the palms, in that they are not produced by the quiet love of perceiving truth and uniting it to its own good, but are the fruits of loyal, zealous obedience to the truths taught by the leaders of the Church as the Lord's instruction.

This is the faith of great numbers in the Christian Church. Their songs of praise are in the same strain with that of the people who went out to meet the Lord, and of their kindred multitude who stood before the throne— they are addressed to the Lord as Savior and King. These are their leaves; and their fruits are the joys of delivering from evil all whom they can bring to look to the Lord with them. The seeds of this fruit are teachings of faith in the Lord, and their stony case is from the truth that there is no Savior but Him.

The Fig Tree

IN MARKED CONTRAST WITH THE UPRIGHT, BRANCHLESS palm, the fig tree, in some of its species, is the most wide-spreading of trees; the famous banyan or pagoda fig of India, sometimes casting a vertical shadow more than fifteen hundred feet in circumference.

The common fig tree, however, whose fruit we use, is a small tree, but with a broad expanse in proportion to its height.

A remarkable characteristic of the fig is that the blossoms are concealed, so that the fruit is popularly supposed to be produced without blossoms. The truth is that the flower stalk, which, in the first crop, pushes itself out in the axil of the leaf bud before the leaf, is hollow, and bears inside a multitude of little flowers, some staminate and some pistillate. When these flowers have matured, the stalk in which they are enclosed expands into a fig—the sweet, nutritious pulp belonging to the stalk itself, and imbedding a multitude of small, dry seed vessels.

This low, spreading, fruitful tree must be representative of principles relating to neighborly uses, not of very interior quality. That the fruit is produced without visible blossoms indicates that the good works to which it corresponds are not preceded by any conscious perception of interior truth. For every spiritual fruit tree springs from a principle of use affectionately received in the mind; its leaves are intelligent perceptions of truth relating to the principle; and the blossoms, which are more delicate leaves, are perceptions of purer, more delightful wisdom concerning its uses. The joy in the perception of the ability of the loved truth to produce good uses expresses itself in the beauty and fragrance of the flower, within which is the beginning of the fruit. The olive tree blossoms with delight in the perception of the Lord's goodness, now given with such fullness that it may be imparted to others; the vine, with the sweet pleasure of communicating the wisdom and kindness of the Divine truth; but the fig is happy in the obscure knowledge that it is right to do good, and in doing kindly works with no perception of what is spiritually wise and useful, and no sense of inflowing life or illustration from the Lord. Hence the fruit seems to belong to the producer himself. The stalk thickens into sweetness, within which the living fruits, which are the Divine precepts of well doing, remain comparatively dry and tasteless.

Such is the fruit of benevolence in children and simple good persons, who receive instruction in moral and benevolent life, accept it as something to be done, without much intelligence about it, and are full of zeal for the works prescribed. Such fruit may appear before the leaf, because it is not dependent upon intelligence. It is the abundant kindliness and morality of simple, obedient goodness.

When our first ancestors lost their spiritual love and intelligence by eating of the tree of knowledge of good and evil, because they were no longer innocent, they were said to be conscious of nakedness; yet they retained their knowledge of the forms of moral life, with which as with fig leaves they clothed themselves (*Divine Providence* §313).

The Jews had in their Scriptures precepts which taught them to consider the poor, to have compassion on the widow and the fatherless, to show hospitality to the stranger, to deal their bread to the hungry, to bring home the poor that were cast out, to undo the heavy burdens, to let the oppressed go free, and to break every yoke; they prided themselves upon their knowledge of the Scriptures and upon their study of them. They were a fig tree glorying in leaves; but when the Lord came seeking fruit upon it, He found none, and presently the fig tree withered away.

But in the prediction of His Second Coming, the Lord gave as a sign the budding of the fig tree: "Behold the fig tree and all the trees; when they now shoot forth, ye see and know of your own selves that summer is now nigh at hand" (Luke 21:29, 30). This was a sign of His coming, because the first effect of His coming would be an active interest in practical philanthropy and in all useful knowledge. Is not this spiritual sign now visible in the immense increase of benevolent feeling and work in our day? In the associations for the relief of the poor, the sick, and insane, the imprisoned, and the unfortunate of every class? In the fact that the pulpits of all the churches are inculcating the precepts of good moral life, instead of the arbitrary dogmas of the last century? And in the advance of scientific knowledge, so rapid as to cover every branch of the tree of science with a growth that almost conceals the stock of a hundred years ago? What possible explanation of this marvelous and sudden development can a fair mind suggest but the nearer approach of the Divine Spirit of wisdom and goodness?

The Pomegranate

THE POMEGRANATE IS:

A fruit-bearing tree, or rather shrub, or the myrtle family, which is cultivated through all the warmer parts of the Old World, from Northern

India through Persia, and in all the countries bordering on the Mediterranean. It is indigenous in North Africa and Southern France, and flourishes in Bermuda and many of the West Indian islands. It is evergreen, and forms rather a collection of small stems ... than a single tree, nor does it often exceed eight or ten feet in height. The leaves are lanceolate, glossy, and small, of a very delicate greenish-red color. ... The bell-shaped blossom is extremely beautiful and conspicuous, varying from scarlet to a deep orange-red, and the fruit, when ripe, is of a bright red color, as large as an orange, and crowned with its calyx, which adds much to its grace of form. ... It continues to throw out a succession of blossoms from March to June. ... There are two sorts cultivated in orchards, the sweet and the sour, contrasting in taste like the orange and lemon, though the appearance of the fruit is precisely similar. The Romans, who introduced the tree from Carthage, gave it the name *punicum malum*, the Carthaginian apple; and our name pomegranate is derived from the Latin "grained apple," from the striking appearance of the bright pink pips, packed in compartments separated by a white membrane, shining like rubies, and beautifully arranged. ...

The bark and the rind of the fruit are powerful astringents, and are used medicinally in the East; but are chiefly valuable as tannin. The rind of the wild pomegranate is still carefully collected in Morocco and the Sahara, and is used exclusively for the preparation of the finest sort of morocco leather, giving it a dull red color. (Tristram, *Natural History of the Bible*)

The pomegranate, from the abundance of its seeds, was regarded in ancient times as an emblem of fruitfulness. The tree upon which it grows is of a humbler kind than any which has so far been mentioned, being scarcely more than a flowering shrub. We should, therefore, look for its correspondence rather among the good things of natural life and knowledge than among those of interior perception. The idea of fruitfulness probably is correct; and the kind of fruitfulness we can learn with some definiteness from the use made of the pomegranate in the furniture of the sacred Tabernacle.

Moses was commanded to cause a robe to be made for Aaron in his ministry before the Lord; and it was said: "Upon the hem of it thou shalt make pomegranates of blue, and of purple, and of scarlet, round about the hem thereof; and bells of gold between them round about; a golden bell and a pomegranate upon the hem of the robe round about. And it shall be upon Aaron to minister; and his sound shall be heard when he goeth in unto the holy place before Jehovah, and when he cometh out, that he die not" (Exodus 28:33–35).

By the garments of Aaron, who represents the ministry of Divine things from the Lord among men, is meant the Divine Truth in the Lord's Word and teachings from it. The hem of this garment is the principles of good life and right morality in which all Divine teachings terminate, and by which they are held firmly together. The pomegranates depending from this hem in colors of truth and love and charity, are representatives of the beautiful life springing from these Christian principles; and the golden bells are teachings of the presence of the Lord, with worship from love for Him—the acknowledgment that the good life is from the Lord (*Arcana Coelestia* §9918, 9921).

Olives are forms of knowledge of the Lord's goodness; grapes are knowledge of the sweetness and spirit of His wisdom; dates are glad experiences of His salvation; figs are fruits of natural kindness and benevolence; and pomegranates represent abundant natural usefulness based upon Christian charity.

The golden candlestick in the tabernacle of the Israelites was ornamented with pomegranates and flowers. Each of the six branches terminated in "three bowls made like unto almonds, a pomegranate and a flower"; and the central shaft in "four bowls made like unto almonds, their pomegranates and their flowers"; and under each pair of branches of the candlestick was a pomegranate (Exodus 25:31–36). The candlestick of pure gold is a representative of the wisdom of the Lord in the heavens and the Church. Its ornaments were pomegranates with their flowers, because that wisdom is the wisdom of usefulness, and its delights are the perceptions of means and opportunities of usefulness. Its branches sprang in pairs from the pomegranates because the Divine wisdom regards equally what is right and what is good, and both rightness and goodness are essential to wise life, and spring from love for wise life.

Various Fruits

IN REGARD TO THE CORRESPONDENCE OF OTHER FRUITS than those which have been mentioned, we have very little instruction from Swedenborg. The following sketches claim no authority but that of reasonableness, so far as they are reasonable.

Oranges are more entirely composed of juice than any of the other fruits except grapes. They are a coarser fruit than grapes, less digestible, more perishable. They yield no spirited wine; but contain some of the same acid as apples (Lindley). They are produced in tropical countries; but are used all over the civilized world. Lindley says:

> The productiveness of the common orange is enormous. A single tree at St. Michael's has been known to produce twenty thousand oranges fit for packing, exclusive of the damaged fruit and the waste, which may be calculated at one third more. (*Vegetable Kingdom*, p. 458)

It is also to be noticed that it is evergreen, and is bearing fruit the whole year round, new blossoms appearing as the former fruit matures.

Evidently oranges are representatives of wisdom of a widely useful and perennially interesting kind. A clue to their exact meaning we find incidentally in Swedenborg. He relates that two angels from the third heaven were sent down to him to show him the form of conjugial love. After some discourse upon the subject, they were recalled, and "were carried along a paved way, through fields of flowers, from which sprung up olives, and trees laden with oranges" (*Conjugial Love* §2). By the olives is meant mutual love received from the Lord; here the inmost mutual love, which is marriage love; and by the trees laden with oranges must be meant wisdom concerning marriage; for this only would be appropriate to the occasion. Orange blossoms,

likewise, are everywhere regarded as the appropriate ornaments of weddings. There is a marriage of red and white
in the color of the orange. Its immense and perennial
fruitfulness represents very fairly the interest with which
wisdom on this subject is acquired and imparted.

The leaves of the tree are jointed, like the leaves of the
rosebush and many other plants, seeming thereby to represent perceptions of complex relations. But the orange
develops only one leaflet; perhaps because the friendship
to which it relates is limited to one.

The cultivation of oranges seems to have been introduced into Europe since the Christian Era began; and it
is at least a coincidence that the idea of the union of
minds in marriage is one of the later growths of Christianity. When the Lord explained to the disciples the wrong
of divorce for idle causes, the disciples replied, "If the case
of the man be so with his wife, it is not good to marry"
(Matthew 19:10). Paul also taught that celibacy is really
preferable to marriage (1 Corinthians 7).

It will be observed that many fruits are of two kinds:
sweet and sour. There are sweet and sour apples, and apricots, sweet and bitter almonds, oranges of every shade of
sweetness, sourness, and bitterness, but in general sweet,
and contrasted with the sourness of lemons and limes.

Sweet fruits represent pleasant encouragement of good;
and tart fruits a sharper and more stimulating wisdom of
the duty and necessity of good life—the most acrid representing a critical censoriousness that is discouraging.
Lemons and limes therefore appear to represent wisdom
that teaches the spiritual necessity of pure and good marriage life.

The common fruit trees throughout the temperate
regions of the earth are apples, pears, quinces, which form

a group by themselves; and peaches, apricots, plums, and cherries, which form another group.

It is uncertain what fruit is meant by the "apple" mentioned in the Canticles,* and also in Joel 1:12. Tristram thinks it cannot be the proper apple, since that fruit "barely exists in the country." The apricot, he thinks, is probably the fruit; as it is most abundant throughout the land, is not mentioned otherwise in the Bible, and meets all the requirements of the context. It is possible that the name is a general one for fragrant, edible fruits, including all that are mentioned above; and also lemons and oranges, and perhaps some others. Gesenius says that the name in Arabic means properly apples, but includes also lemons, peaches, apricots, etc. The Latin word *malum* has a similar general significance, standing for "any tree fruit fleshy on the outside, and having a kernel within; hence [besides apples] used also of quinces, pomegranates, peaches, oranges, lemons, etc." (Andrews, *Latin Lexicon*).

All these are juicy fruits, not oil-yielding, and on this account, like grapes, they represent some pleasant truth matured by thoughtful experience; though no one of them bears so generously nor produces so noble wine as the vine.

A marked division among them appears upon slight attention. The apples, pears, and quinces are many-seeded fruits, with firm flesh composed of the thickened calyx and stem. Peaches, apricots, and others of their family, have each a single hard stone, enclosed in a more tender and juicy pulp, which is formed from the pistil itself. Oranges, lemons, and limes differ from both in having a thick, leathery rind, in which, as in the leaves, there is a

---

* The Song of Solomon.

considerable quantity of oil; and, while they have many seeds, they have no core, but are pulpy throughout, like berries; in this particular resembling grapes.

In regard to the meaning of the apple, Mythology gives us a curious and valuable suggestion. According to Mr. Murray, *Nemesis* was the goddess of punishment:

> A mysterious power, watching over the propriety of life, she was conceived as shaping the demeanor of men in their times of prosperity, punishing crime, taking luck from the unworthy, tracking every wrong to its doer, and keeping society in equipoise. . . . Among her several attributes were a wheel, to indicate the speed of her punishments, a balance, a bridle, a yoke, a rudder, a lash, a sword and *an apple branch.* (*Manual of Mythology*, p. 217)

The wisdom of the proprieties of life, or of morals and manners, seems to answer well to the characteristics of the apple. Its goodness is superficial, as the flesh of the apple is the thickened stem and casing. Its sharp or kindly criticism forms as large a part of social communications as the flesh and juice of the apple do of daily food. And not sooner does the juice of the apple turn to vinegar than critical thoughts once expressed turn to sharp censure. In the freshness of the occasion that called them forth they may be only bright and stimulating; but it is remarkable how little repetition or thinking over they will bear before all the kindliness is gone out of them, and only sharp censure is left. If pure and true, this may still be useful in moderate quantity.

The vinegar of the Bible is the vinegar of grapes, and represents truth of life loved not from charity and sweet affection, but from a censorious spirit; it may be from a love of chastening evil, or from a desire to condemn others for the sake of exalting oneself. The Lord taught pure truth from love for the goodness and happiness to which it leads. His followers, in countries called Christian, have turned the truth into censures and threats, by which they oppress and rule over men. It was the perception of the coming perversion of His teachings that was represented by His tasting of the vinegar upon the cross (*Apocalypse Explained* §386).

The pear is a more luscious and tender fruit than the apple, of the same kind. It seems to represent the wisdom of polite and elegant manners. The thorniness of the ungrafted tree may represent the exclusiveness of an unregenerate love of polite manners.

Quinces grow on bushes, not trees, and are not eatable till cooked and much sweetened. Their growth, upon low, straggling stems, shows their correspondence with something without elevation or unity—to rules of society, rather than to intelligently understood general principles of conduct. Such knowledge of rules—unbearable if applied crudely—held pleasantly, with great kindness, makes a somewhat elegant and stimulating entertainment.

These three, in their many seeds, their bright, sharp juice, and their construction out of the stem and thickened calyx, are forms of truth applied in their several ways to the morals and manners of the community.

The softer, sweeter, single-seeded group, are forms of sweeter, kinder manners from a principle of charity. The fruits of the apple kind represent a knowledge of what is true and right and reasonable in natural life; but these of the peach family represent a knowledge of what makes a good home, a good neighborhood, a pleasant school, springing from a single-hearted enjoyment in goodness. The rules and principles of social life are many, like apple seeds; its goodness, with the perception thereof, is single, like the stone of a peach.

The general necessity for moral goodness forms a stony wall about its seed; but no such absolute certainty encompasses the particular principles.

The wooliness of most peaches is a curious confirmation of their correspondence with a knowledge of kind and affectionate manners.

Nectarines are only a smooth variety of peach.

Apricots and plums are perhaps related to peaches somewhat as pears are to apples. Cherries are sometimes grouped with plums, and sometimes in a distinct genus; and from their small size, early ripening, and clustered arrangement, appear to relate to the pleasures of childhood's social life.

The Nut Trees

Almonds

ANOTHER APPARENTLY VERY DIFFERENT FRUIT, BUT OF THE same genus with the peach, is the almond.

Almonds are stones of peaches made sweet and eatable in themselves, but not encompassed with sweet pulp. They are not quickly perishable as is the juicy fruit; and in this respect, as well as in their dry nutritious quality, they partake of the character of the grains.

Taking the peach as a type of works of affection, the seeds are principles of the duty of charity by which such works are multiplied. And almonds are these principles of charity lived from love for their own goodness. In peaches the seed is out of sight, and the sweet pulp appears to be the fruit. In almonds the seed is the fruit. In the works represented by peaches, there must be much expression of neighborly affection; but in the almonds there is no demonstrativeness, only a quiet doing of good works as a loved duty.

Peaches, from their perishableness and juiciness, suggest occasional kind hospitalities and other expressions of affectionate interest to friends and neighbors; the drier almonds represent quiet daily service from the duty of love.

The priesthood of Aaron and his sons represented the ministry of the goodness of the Lord among men, and especially the living of a life of charity to lead men in the way to heaven. Therefore, when the rods of the several tribes were laid up before the Lord, Aaron's rod, for the tribe of Levi, blossomed, and brought forth almonds, which represented the use to which he and his tribe were appointed.

The Hebrew name for the almond is "the watchful," a name said to be conferred because its pretty pink flowers open their eyes so early in the winter, in which the peaches also resemble them. And, spiritually, the love of a life of charity is ever awake to its opportunities.

The Lord said to Jeremiah, whom He was sending to reprove the people for their many sins, "What seest thou, Jeremiah?" And when Jeremiah replied "An almond rod," the Lord explained it as an emblem of Himself as to His Divine watchfulness to lead men in the heavenly way: "Thou doest well in seeing; for watchful am I over my words to do them" (Jeremiah 1:11, 12).

Perhaps we can now see why the burners of the golden candlestick were "made like unto almonds"; for the candlestick is a representative of the Divine wisdom in the Church, and the ultimations of this are teachings of the duties of charity.

In the present which Jacob sent to Egypt by his sons, to the almonds were added "pistacia nuts." In explaining this, Swedenborg says that the almonds represent "goods of life corresponding to the truths of interior natural good"; and the pistacia nuts, which he calls terebinth, represent "goods of life corresponding to the truths of exterior natural good" (*Arcana Coelestia* §5622). That is, the almonds are duties of real charity, and the pistacia nuts of natural pleasantness.

The pistacia tree is related to the terebinth, which will be described presently; also to a large group of trees yielding varnishes, and to the poisonous rhus, or sumac, which produces painful inflammation of the skin.

Beech Trees

THE SIGNIFICATION OF ALMONDS, AS PRINCIPLES OF CHARity in life, suggests the idea that other nuts may represent the living of other good principles, and the trees themselves the knowledge of them.

A solitary beech is a wide-spreading, symmetrical tree; but in the forests it sometimes attains a considerable height. Its bark is smooth, which, together with the polish and integrity of the leaves, gives an impression of extreme cleanliness. Its nuts are very oily, sharply three-sided, growing in pairs in bristly burs.

The cleanliness of the tree suggests that the principle which it represents is a principle of purity. The oil of the fruit shows that the corresponding works are works of love. Their growing in pairs indicates that they relate to marriage—all of which is confirmed and made definite by what Swedenborg says of them in the other world. In the description of the palace representing conjugial love in the three planes of the mind, he relates that around the palace were olive, palm, and beech trees; which three, he says, represent the truths of conjugial love in the celestial, spiritual and natural planes of the mind respectively (*Conjugial Love* §270). The olive, as we have seen, represents the perception and knowledge of the Lord's love, which, when retrieved, manifests itself as mutual love, and especially as the sweetest form of mutual love, which is conjugial love. The palm also, in representing a knowledge of the Lord's salvation, relates especially to salvation from the natural passions of youth, and to the consequent reception of a pure-hearted love for marriage. And the beech must represent a knowledge of the *duty* of singleness in marriage. The three-sided nuts, full of pleasant oil, and growing, a pair close together within each smooth-lined bristly bur, are as pretty an image as a plant can show of life according to this principle.

Chestnuts

IN HIS JOURNEY TO THE PEOPLE OF THE IRON AGE,* SWE-denborg approached them, with the accompanying angel, through "a forest consisting of beeches, chestnuts, and oaks" (*Conjugial Love* §78). These seem to have been situated between the people of the Copper Age and those of the Iron, and to have partaken of the quality, at least as to the beeches, of the nobler age; for the Iron people did not live in singleness of marriage. So likewise in approaching the men of the Copper Age, he entered their heaven from the south, where he found "a magnificent grove of palms and laurels," which certainly partake of the intelligent quality of the earlier Silver Age.

* This refers not to our modern archaeological idea of the Iron Age, but to Swedenborg's division of history into epochs identified with particular churches. The Golden Age refers to the Most Ancient Church, which existed from the time of Adam to the time of Moses; the Silver Age and the Copper (or Bronze) Age took place during the time of the Ancient Church, from Noah to Moses; and the Iron Age is the third church, also called the Jewish or Israelitish Church, which spans the time from Moses receiving the Ten Commandments to the coming of Jesus Christ.

The statement first mentioned is interesting from its association of the chestnut and the oak with the beeches. They form one family, with marked differences. The chestnut, which comes nearest to the beech, is distinguished from it for our purpose by the irregular number of nuts, from one to three in each bur, by the larger size of the nuts, and by the smaller quantity of oil in them. The trees are cultivated for their fruit and also for their wood, which is less solid than that of the beech, but is exceedingly durable, especially as compared with other hardwoods, when in or near the ground; for which reason it is much used for fences and for sills of houses.

It evidently represents some kind of knowledge of natural life. And as the pair of oily beech nuts represent a knowledge of the duty of singleness in marriage, the chestnuts, of indefinite number, may represent the kindred duty of care for children. The warmly lined bur, so soft within and prickly without, suggests a comfortable and well-protected home; and is a very perfect representative of the paternal feeling which would guard the children from every hurtful approach till they arrive at maturity. This is very similar to the instinct of protection around one's marriage life, as the bur of the chestnut resembles that of the beech.

The sharp angles of the beech nut indicate the perfect definiteness of the law of singleness which it represents; and the rounder, more irregular forms of the chestnuts express the greater indefiniteness and variety of principles of education.

The wide spread of the branches, and the extreme age of some chestnuts, shows the comprehensiveness and permanence of some principles of education. The durability of the wood in the ground represents the endurance of the principles when exposed to the experiences of the world—parents carrying out good principles for their children's sake much more patiently than they will for their own; whence their use as foundation timbers for our homes.

The Oak

THE OAK WOULD SEEM TO BELONG WITH PECULIAR APPRO-priateness to the people of an Iron Age.[1] More than any other family of trees it seems to answer in the vegetable kingdom to the iron of the mineral. "Strong as an oak" and "tough as an oak" are common expressions which are entirely justified by the character of the tree.

> The main root of the oak, where the soil is favorable, descends to a great depth compared with its height, especially in young trees, and it stretches to a distance horizontally—and that at a considerable depth—equal to the spread of the branches; thus taking a stronger hold of the earth than any other tree of the forest. It does not often tower upwards to so magnificent a height as many other trees; but, when standing alone, it throws out its mighty arms with an air of force and grandeur which has made it everywhere to be considered the fittest emblem of strength and power of resistance. The great value of the oak, in all countries, is for its wood. It is applied to a greater variety of important purposes than that of any other tree. . . . For strength, hard-

---

1. See the preceding article, under "Chestnuts."

ness, toughness, and durableness united, it is unsurpassed; although each of these properties singly is found to a greater degree in some other wood." (Emerson's *Trees and Shrubs of Massachusetts*, pp. 137, 138)

The first knowledge of good and evil, right and wrong which a child has, is not an interior, rational knowledge, but a knowledge of the statements and teachings which are the results of thought. There is such a thing as thinking rationally from a knowledge of the Divine standards of right, and, from that rational thought, deducing rules or formulas of speech and action, relating to practical questions of every kind. A child's first knowledge is a knowledge of such formulas, not thought out rationally by him, but learned from others with a child's intelligence, and held with great tenacity and stiffness, because they are the strength of his life. When Abram first entered the land of Canaan, he dwelt in the oak grove of Moreh; and afterwards in the oak grove of Mamre. And this Swedenborg interprets as meaning that when the Lord departed from the natural states into which He was born, and began to learn of Divine and heavenly states, His first knowledge was of this childlike kind. The things first learned are like oaks, he says, "on account of the intertwined branches of the oak" (*Arcana Coelestia* §1443). They are like oaks also in the strength and tenacity with which they are held. And their fruits, or the works done from such knowledge of right and wrong, are like the somewhat bitter, but not innutritious, acorns.

It is interesting to note the affinity which the acid of oak galls and oak bark has for iron. The acid of the oak must represent a zeal for formulating, or for fixing and remembering in set forms; for the whole tree represents a knowledge of and a love for such forms. Iron is the representative of ultimate truth in which all life rests. This the zeal for formulating seizes upon as the very means of making knowledge fixed and definite; as the oak acid unites with the iron to make ink, with which all knowledge is written down in fixed and enduring forms.

The acid of oak bark unites in the same way with the skins of animals, to make leather. For the skins of animals represent the usual manifestations and descriptions of the natural affections; of which the zeal for formulating makes a clothing of manners, according to the customs of the world, fitted to bear hard knocks, and to conceal and protect the sensitive feelings within it.

The Divine Truth in the lowest form of definite laws and customs is as it is usually presented in the Old Testament, and as it was revealed by living voice from Mount Sinai to the Israelites. This was the character of the Dispensation of which the Israelites constituted the center. In the circumferences of the Dispensation, accordingly, among the Gentile nations, oracles were established in oak groves, where men inquired the will of the gods, and where no doubt they received instruction from the spiritual world, adapted to their state. Zeus, the great god of the Greeks, we are told, "at Dodona in Epirus, revealed his will towards men, and the incidents of their future life, in the rustling of the branches of a holy oak" (Murray, p. 48). "The oak and the olive, of all the trees of the earth . . . were most sacred to him" (p. 50); the olive because it represented perceptions of the love of God in the inmost of the mind, and the oak because it represented the perception of His will in ultimates. Therefore, also, "as god of Dodona, he wears a wreath of oak leaves, and as Olympic god, a wreath of the sacred olive of Olympia" (p. 51).

The Terebinth

FROM THE HEBREW ROOT SIGNIFYING "MIGHTY" ARE DERIVED several names which are usually translated "oak," or "plane," in our Bible. All of them, however, appear to stand for trees remarkable for size and strength. There is a general agreement among interpreters that a part of these names refer to the *terebinth* tree, as they are translated in the Septuagint. The names seem to be used sometimes interchangeably (as in Genesis 25:4; Joshua 24:26; Judges 9:6), probably because all the trees indicated by them have a similar general appearance and a like correspondence, of course with a difference; but sometimes they are carefully distinguished, as in Isaiah 6:13.

Tristram says of the terebinth:

> It is the *Pistacia Terebinthus* of botanists . . . well known in the Greek Islands as the turpentine tree. In Chios, especially, a considerable quantity of turpentine is extracted from it by tapping the trunk; but this is not practiced in Palestine, where the inhabitants seem to be ignorant of its commercial value. It is a very common tree in the southern and eastern parts of the country, being generally found in situations too warm or dry for the oak, whose place it there supplies, and which it much resembles in general appearance at a distance. It is seldom seen in clumps or groves, never in forests, but stands isolated and weird-like in some bare ravine or on a hillside, where nothing else towers above the low brushwood. When it sheds its leaves at the beginning of winter, it still more recalls the familiar English oak, with its short and gnarled trunk,

spreading and irregular limbs, and small twigs. . . . Many terebinths remain to this day objects of veneration in their neighborhood; and the favorite burying place of the Bedouin sheik is under a soli - tary tree. Eastern travelers will recall the "Mother of Rags" on the outskirts of the desert—a terebinth covered with the votive offerings of superstition or affection. The terebinth of Mamre, or its lineal successor, remained from the days of Abraham till the fourth century of the Christian Era; and on its site Constantine erected a Christian church, the ruins of which still remain." (*Natural History of the Bible*, Article: "Teil Tree")

As ordinarily met with today, the terebinth attains the stature of thirty or thirty-five feet. The root is substantial, and penetrates deeply into the ground; the boughs spread widely, and at a considerable angle, and being clothed, except in winter, with dark and shining foliage, the tree presents, during the larger portion of the year, a beautiful and conspicuous spectacle. The reddish hue of the branches and of the petioles, especially while the parts are young, contributes to the pleasing effect. The leaves, which individually are three or four inches long, consist of about seven ovate-lanceolate leaf - lets disposed in a pinnate manner. The flowers are borne in racemes, and though small and insignif - icant, somewhat like those of the grapevine, are pretty, being yellowish, with crimson stigmas. In due time, they are succeeded by dark blue drupes, the size of peas, but ovoid, in substance dry, and containing each a solitary and bony seed, the kernel of which is oleaginous and edible. The foliage and the flowers alike evolve a resinous odor, which is diffused like that of sweetbriar, especially towards evening, and when the day has been warm. Though deciduous, the terebinth is thus a tree of many attractions. . . . In the island of Scio, the resinous matter which diffuses the scent is collected in quantity by means of incisions made in the trunk. When extracted, it yields an odor resembling that of jessamine flowers, or the citron, and gradually hardens into a translucent solid—the Chian turpentine of commerce. (Grindon, *Scripture Botany*)

Lindley calls this turpentine "a limpid, fragrant, balsamic resin, with an odor between lemon and fennel" (*Vegetable Kingdom*, p. 467). He says, also, that trees of this family yield valuable varnishes, and that many members of the family are highly poisonous; among which are our poisonous ivy and sumac, which induce, and also relieve, painful skin and rheumatic diseases.

As the oak represents a knowledge of natural teachings of right and wrong, as applied to the affairs of life, the terebinth seems to represent a knowledge of similar teachings which conduce to peace, to smoothness of living in society, and to the removal of irritation. Its balsamic resin shows the pleasant soothing thought of the intelligence which it represents; and the affection in it is further indicated by the combustible, heat-giving power of the resin. The use of kindred resins for varnishes points in the same direction; and it is manifest that the knowledge of human infirmities which is necessary to adjust our social relations to smooth and peaceful working, if used perversely, has power to produce irritation and inability to work at all, which appears to be represented by the highly poisonous effects, especially upon the skin, produced by some plants of the family.

Its representation is parallel with that of the oak; the one relating to what is right, and the other to what is good, on the same plane. The dry stone fruit of the terebinth further indicates its representation of a knowledge of what is good. The composite character of its leaves may indicate the perception of complex relations, as the strongly lobed oak leaves seem to represent a perception of the application of principles of right in various directions.

Cone-Bearing Trees

Besides the nut trees, there are many trees that bear no edible fruit, but are valuable for timber and for beauty and healthfulness. They therefore represent, not duties, nor uses, but knowledge which in itself is useful. They are of every degree of nobility, from the cedar to the poplar, and represent knowledge of human life of every grade, from a knowledge of heaven and of the immortality of the soul to a knowledge of what people say and of the fashions.

Of the timber trees mentioned in the Bible, the most prominent is the Cedar of Lebanon.

The Cedar of Lebanon

It was the grandest tree known to Solomon; for he "spake of trees, from the cedar tree that is in Lebanon, even unto the hyssop that springeth out of the wall" (1 Kings 4:33). It was both tall and wide-spreading; for Isaiah speaks of "the cedars of Lebanon, that are high and lifted up" (Isaiah 2:13); and Ezekiel says, "Behold, the Assyrian was a cedar in Lebanon with fair branches, and thickness of shadowing, and of a high stature; and his top was among the thick boughs. The waters made him great, the deep set him up on high with her rivers running about his plants. ... Therefore his height was exalted above all the trees of the field, and his boughs were multiplied, and his branches became long because of the multitude of waters. ... All the fowls of heaven made their nests in his boughs, and under his branches did all the beasts of the field bring forth their young, and under his shadow dwelt all great nations" (Ezekiel 31:3–6).

The cedars now known upon Lebanon do not attain so magnificent proportions as this description would imply; but it is probable that the finest parts of the Lebanon forest are gone, and that the scanty groves now remaining, though giving us the general character of the trees, do not present their finest development. The cedars of the Himalaya, regarded as a variety of the same species, are said to attain a height of two hundred and fifty feet, and a circumference of thirty-nine feet. Of the Lebanon cedars, Mr. Grindon writes: "What is wanting in stature is compensated by the girth of the trunk, the noble proportions and the prodigious size and expansion of the principal boughs, which, in fine examples, are themselves equal to the whole of many a forest tree. These huge limbs spread to so great a distance that when a cedar stands isolated upon the sward, a space is overshadowed which in area considerably exceeds the vertical measure. They strike out, moreover, in distinct horizontal stages, causing the tree to appear stratified."

This last-mentioned characteristic is strongly marked in the photographs of the cedars, and is mentioned by many observers. Mr. Thompson says: "The branches are thrown out horizontally from the parent trunk. These again part into limbs which preserve the same horizontal direction, and so on down to the minutest twigs, and even the arrangement of the clustered leaves has the same general tendency. Climb into one, and you are delighted with a succession of verdant floors spread around the trunk, and gradually narrowing as you ascend. The beautiful cones seem to stand upon, or rise out of, this green flooring" (*The Land and the Book*, i. 297). The writer in Baedeker's Guide-Book compares these successive strata of foliage to "small patches of meadow," out of which the cones grow.

The leaves of the tree grow in clusters like those of the larch, but grow so thick upon the numerous twigs as to make a solid mat of foliage, casting a dense shadow. Unlike the larch, they are evergreen. Of the resinous quality of the tree, Mr. Thompson says: "The wood, bark, cones, and even leaves of the cedar, are saturated, so to speak, with resin. The *heart* has the red cedar color, but the exterior is whitish. It is certainly a very durable wood, but is not fine-grained nor sufficiently compact to take a high polish; for ordinary architectural purposes, however, it is perhaps the best there is in the country" (p. 297).

The rapidly-grown wood of the English specimens is described as worthless for building purposes. But there is much evidence that the wood of the mountains is durable, pleasing in color, and fragrant. Mr. Tristram testifies that "the wood of the mountain-grown cedar of Lebanon is much closer in grain and darker in color than that of trees grown in England" (*Natural History of the Bible*, 343). A small piece in my possession closely resembles in color, fragrance, and texture the wood of our American Arbor Vitæ (*Thuya Occidentalis*), the "white cedar" of Maine, which, though not a tough wood, is noted for durability.

In looking for the mental correlative of this noble tree, the point of attention must be the representation of those successive platforms of verdure, mounting higher and higher into the heavens, which are the most striking characteristics of the tree.

The spiritual tree also must extend its branches, put forth leaves, and mature its fruit on successively interior planes of the mind. It must be acquainted with both natural and spiritual things, and recognize their distinctness as well as their unity. We need not look farther to recognize the truth of Swedenborg's explanation: "By Ashur, the cedar in Lebanon, is signified the rational mind, which is formed from natural knowledge on the one part, and from the influx of spiritual truth on the other" (*Apocalypse Explained* §650).

The cedar of the mind extends its branches of knowledge widely and compactly over the domain of natural life, and another series of branches, with almost equal comprehensiveness, among the things of spiritual life; it knows the nature of spiritual love, and distinguishes clearly between the affections which are of God, and those which are natural to men; and its top reaches even to that inmost conscious plane of the mind in which the presence of the Lord Himself, with its infinite variety, is the holy and beautiful object of knowledge. In Swedenborg's journey to the heaven of the Golden Age, the heaven nearest the Lord and most filled with His influence, he came at length to a grove of tall cedars, with some eagles upon their branches; upon seeing which, the angel guide said, "We are now upon the mountain, not far from the top"; "and," Swedenborg adds, "we went on, and behold, behind the grove was a circular plain, where lambs were pasturing, which were forms representative of the state of innocence and peace of the inhabitants of the mountain" (*Conjugial Love* §75).

The cedars reached *to* that inmost heaven; and they were representatives of the rational intelligence which attains to a perception of its innocent quality. This is not the wisdom of that heaven, which is only exquisite perceptions of the Lord's love; but it is the wisdom of the next, or the Noahtic heaven, which touches upon it.

"A spiritual rational Church," Swedenborg says the cedars represent, "such as was the Church among the ancients after the flood" (*Apocalypse Explained* §1100). "The study of our age," these ancients told him, "was the study of truths by which we had intelligence; this was the study of our souls and minds, but the study of our bodily senses was the representations of truths in forms, and a knowledge of correspondences conjoined the sensations of our bodies with the perceptions of our minds, and procured for us intelligence" (*Conjugial Love* §76).

A similar spiritual state is represented by Solomon's temple, which was lined throughout with cedar of Lebanon. For a house is a natural representative of a state of life; if a dwelling house, it represents a state of living; if a temple, a state of worship. The lining of Solomon's temple with cedar, therefore, signifies that the state of worship represented by the temple is interiorly a state of spiritual rationality, which discriminates between spiritual and natural, understands the spiritual truth taught by the natural representatives of the Word and of Nature, and loves it for the sake of good spiritual life.

In Ezekiel it is promised by the Lord that such intelligence shall again take root in the earth in a Church which shall interiorly love the Lord and live in charity, and that its branches shall extend through the several planes of the mind, and give homes to all who delight in intelligent spiritual thought. "Thus saith the Lord Jehovah; I will also take of the highest branch of the high cedar, and will set it; I will crop off from the top of his young twigs a tender one, and will plant it upon a high mountain and eminent: in the mountains of the height of Israel will I plant it; and it shall bring forth boughs, and bear fruit, and be a goodly cedar; and under it shall dwell all fowl of every wing: in the shadow of the branches thereof shall they dwell" (Ezekiel 17:22, 23).

The promise has not yet been fulfilled, it is true; but the branch is set, and we wait only for its development. Upon a certain occasion, in the spiritual world, Swedenborg says, "I saw a cedar table, upon which was a book, under a green olive tree, whose trunk was entwined with a vine. I looked, and behold it was a book written by me, called *Angelic Wisdom concerning the Divine Love and the Divine Wisdom*, and also *Concerning the Divine Providence*; and I said [to the good spirits with whom he was talking] that it was fully shown in that book that man is an organ recipient of life, and not life" (*Apocalypse Revealed* §875).

The olive tree is the growing perception of the Lord's love; the vine is the perception of His wisdom of life; both of which are abundant in the heavenly states to which Swedenborg leads us. And, under these, just such angelic philosophy as a living cedar represents is contained in the very book which Swedenborg saw appropriately borne upon the wood of a cedar tree.

The fragrance of the cedar should not be passed without mention, though the general subject of fragrant materials will receive more attention presently. By odors we perceive the interior quality of a substance, whether it be sweet or foul, and recognize its agreement with our life; therefore it is said of sacrifices which had a good representation, that Jehovah smelled a sweet savor from them. The sweet odors of flowers and fruits show the agreement of their life with pleasant life in us, and thus are expressions to us of the sweetness and gladness of their life. The fragrance of the cedar wood, therefore, represents the delightfulness of such knowledge as is signified by the cedar; for there are differences in the delightfulness of knowledge.

The fragrance of wood depends chiefly upon the essential oil and the resin it contains. Some wood has much of these, and some scarcely any. There are trees beautiful to the sight, but with watery sap and no fragrance, which evidently represent knowledge which is intellectually beautiful and satisfactory, but which stirs no deep affections. But the trees whose sap is composed of fragrant resins and oils represent knowledge that appeals to the heart rather than to the understanding—knowledge that is good and delightful to the life, as distinguished from that which is true and right. As for the cedar, we shall find woods more remarkable for their sweet oils and resins; yet the tree that adequately represents the delightfulness of spiritual rationality, the spiritual joy of the mind which discerns between spiritual and natural, and perceives intelligently the correspondence between them, certainly cannot be lacking in fragrance.

The Sequoias

THE GREAT *SEQUOIAS* OF CALIFORNIA ARE ARRANGED BY Dr. Gray between the cedars of Lebanon and the cypress. Their prodigious height and size and very great longevity indicate their correspondence with vast and comprehensive ideas, including all planes of human life; and their discovery on the extreme west of the continent, as the wave of habitation completed the circuit of the earth, suggests *the unity of mankind* as the possible subject. May it not be that the larger of the two species represents a knowledge of the unity of Divine revelations; and the smaller, the unity of the Churches or races formed by these revelations?

The Cypress

ASSOCIATED WITH THE CEDARS IN THE BUILDING OF SOLomon's temple was the wood called, in our translation, "fir." Probably this, like the "cedar," is a general term, including several kinds of trees. The cypress, the juniper, and pines of several species are selected respectively by various authors as probably the tree that is meant.

Mr. Grindon, who, following Dr. Royle, accepts the cypress as the "fir" of the English Bible, thus pleasantly describes it:

> In general figure, this beautiful tree corresponds with the Lombardy poplar, for which, in pictures of Oriental landscape, it appears to be not uncom - monly mistaken. The branches are erect, close to the main stem, and almost in a line with it, so that, from a somewhat rounded base, it tapers gracefully to a point, the stature, in full-grown individuals, being fifty or sixty feet. The leaves, which endure for six or seven years, are extremely minute, and pressed so close to the surface of the twigs that they

are scarcely distinguishable; the innumerable but trifling flowers appear in spring; the fruit is a curious modification of the cone, nearly globular, and technically called a "galbulus." Everywhere in the Greek Archipelago, also in Asia Minor and in Syria, the lofty and evergreen spires are conspicuous at all seasons. . . . The wood of the cypress is of remarkably fine and close grain, fragrant, very durable, and of a pleasing reddish hue, which Pliny says is never lost. The same author states that the doors of the famous temple of the Ephesian Diana were constructed of cypress, and that, after the lapse of four hundred years, they still seemed new (xvi. 79). He further states that the cypress statue of Jupiter in the capital, which had existed six hundred years, showed not a symptom of decay. Horace says that writings worthy of being handed down to remote posterity are, or ought to be, preserved in cabinets made of the same (*Ars Poetica*, 332).

"The gates of Constantinople," also, according to Lindley (*Vegetable Kingdom*, p. 228), "famous for having stood from the time of Constantine to that of Pope Eugene IV, a period of eleven hundred years, were of cypress."

From ancient days cypresses have been planted by graves and in cemeteries, representing, in the upward pointing of every shoot and leaf, and the fragrant, enduring wood, a knowledge of immortal life with God in heaven. It is only since the knowledge of the spiritual world was lost that it came to be associated with sadness. "By the ancients," Mr. Emerson says, "the cypress was considered an emblem of immortality; with the moderns, it is emblematical of sadness and mourning."

It recovers its cheerfulness of aspect the moment we dissociate it from the grave, and think of its graceful plumes as typifying our knowledge of immortal life in heaven. But whether this knowledge be the proper door and floor of the temple of the Lord, perhaps we can judge better after comparison with kindred knowledge.

The Juniper

ABUNDANT UPON MT. LEBANON IS A TALL JUNIPER, AKIN to our red cedar, which so nearly resembles the cypress as to be mistaken for it by some writers. (See *Bible Dictionary*, Article: "Cypress.")

The juniper appears to have been used for sacred purposes from remote antiquity. "That under the name of kedros it was burned for the sake of its perfume, or as incense, by the ancient Greeks, appears from Homer's account of the island abode of Calypso (Od. v. 60), and it would appear to be the same to which Pliny refers when he says that 'the wood lasts forever,' and that 'it has long been employed for making statues of the gods' (xiii. 11)" (Grindon). "The red heartwood of the tall, fragrant juniper of Lebanon was no doubt extensively used in the building of the temple," says the *Bible Dictionary*, supporting its assertion by the Septuagint adoption of the juniper, instead of the fir of our English Bible.

The family is so important that, as I can find no full description of the tall juniper of Palestine, I will quote at some length from Mr. Emerson's description of our red cedar *(Juniperus Virginiana)* which probably is equally applicable to the other in its general statements.

"This is usually," he says, "a ragged-looking tree. . . . Surrounded by other trees in a wood, it has a smooth, clear trunk for twelve or fifteen feet and a handsome spiry head. On the rocks it assumes every variety of form, round-headed, irregular, or cone-shaped, sometimes not without beauty. . . . From the exposed situations in which the red cedar grows, it often has to assume fantastic shapes."

Mr. Emerson describes a tree exposed to winds from the sea, with the trunk "much bent, and all the branches violently twisted landward"; and another near the same place, which "lies prostrate on the rock from beneath which it springs. It has a circumference of five feet three inches as near the root as it can be measured, and six feet eight inches at the largest part free from branches. These, numerous, crowded, and matted, bend down like a penthouse over the side of the rock. Others are seen on the same road as if crouching behind walls, rising higher and higher as they recede from the walls, and forming protected, sunny spots for sheep to lie in."

He endorses the statement by Dr. Elliot that "those which grow along the sea coast, with their roots partially immersed in salt water, though smaller in their dimensions, are much more durable than those which inhabit the forests. Often when surrounded and finally destroyed by the encroachments of the salt water, their bodies remain in the marshes for an indefinite period . . . and seem to molder away like rocks, rather than decay like a vegetable product."

"The wood is light, close-grained, smooth and compact, and possessed of great durability. The agreeable and permanent odor recommends it for certain uses, as that of making pencils, and the bottoms of small boxes and drawers, the aroma making it a safeguard against insects. The sapwood is white, but the heartwood of a beautiful red, whence is derived its name."

The cone which we should expect to find for its fruit is transformed by the union of its small, fleshy scales into a little berry, which is a favorite winter food of some birds, especially our robins, or domestic thrushes. "The barren and fertile flowers are on different trees, rarely on the same" (Emerson). The tree "has a geographical range equal, perhaps superior, to that of any other tree known."

Young junipers growing in favorable places are scarcely distinguishable in general appearance from young cypresses. They have a similar upward tendency of every twig, the slender topmost shoot, though tossed by every breath, yet pointing straight heavenward as fast as it gathers strength; their close, fine foliage is similar in effect, and also the reddish, stringy bark. The juniper, however, has more tendency to spread than the cypress, and is much more affected in its form by circumstances. If the cypress represents our knowledge of immortal life with God in heaven, the juniper seems to represent a knowledge of His providence upon earth. It flourishes, if permitted, and becomes a handsome tree, in favored soils and climates; but more frequently it springs from barren hills and broken cliffs, into the crevices of which it pushes its roots deep, submitting them to a degree of compression which flattens and knots them almost beyond recognition as roots; and under these hard circumstances, its red, fragrant heart only grows the redder and sweeter.

Scraggy the patient tree often is to the last degree, and of great variety of form (could a knowledge of the ways of Providence in such a world as this be always symmetrical and uniform?), but it all the more perfectly represents those lives, broken by toil and hardship, which contain the sweet recognition of a kind Father's hand always with them, providing better things than they would have sought for themselves. Especially touching in this light are those bent and deformed watchers by the sea, which, almost prostrate from long-continued yielding to the storms, yet more than others attain strong hearts and patient endurance.

> They that go down to the sea in ships, that do business in great waters, these see the works of Jehovah, and His wonders in the deep. (Psalm 107:23, 24)

Returning now to the question of the trees mentioned in the Bible, we read in 2 Samuel 6:5 that when the Ark was brought up from Baale of Judah, where it had long remained after its captivity in Philistia, "David and all the house of Israel played before Jehovah on all manner of fir wood, even on harps and on psalteries, and on timbrels, and on cornets, and on cymbals." The wood of trees represents the goodness acquired by thinking the truth to which the trees correspond, whence comes the power and affection for perceiving more. The music expresses the sentiments of the players, which in this instance were those of thankfulness for the manifest presence of the Lord once more among them, and for deliverance and safety from their enemies.

Admitting, then, the probability that the "fir" of Scripture includes several trees, in this instance the juniper seems to represent the experience from which sprang the music, better even than the cypress.

As to the outer doors and the floor of Solomon's Temple, which are said to have been made of "fir," the walls being lined with cedar—the temple, as has been said, represents a state of spiritual wisdom and charity; and, in the uncertainty as to the kind of wood intended, it seems necessary to inquire through which, if either, of the kinds of knowledge that have been described, we are introduced into such a state of spiritual intelligence.

I would not confirm an opinion without more thorough information; but it may be safe to admit that the eyes of many are opened to the reality of spiritual things when their friends pass into the spiritual world, and the certainty of their immortal existence comes home to them. It is also true that many, perhaps most, persons are brought to perceive spiritual things clearly through a sense of the presence of the Lord with them, caring for them, protecting them, and leading them out of evil to good. The two kinds of knowledge, though distinct, are parts of one group, which is the knowledge of the omnipresent providence of the Lord; and though one relates especially to the future life, and the other to the present life, neither is complete without the other. It may, therefore, be allowable, until we have further information, to rest in the idea that the general Hebrew term includes both trees, and possibly others that are nearly related.

It is interesting to note in relation to the doors and walls of the temple, that upon them were carved "cherubim and palm trees, and opening flowers"; the cherubim to represent good love from the Lord, the palms to represent salvation by Him from evil, and the opening flowers to represent the new delight in the perception of spiritual truth; all of which seem just the appropriate ornaments of the state and of the knowledge which have been described.

There is another species of juniper, the *Juniperus Communis*, which lies close to the ground, spreading in a thick mat sometimes twenty feet in diameter, and multiplying so greatly as to be a serious injury to the pastures, at the same time that it is almost useless in itself. This appears to represent a knowledge of Divine Providence applied to outward events without interior elevation or intelligence. It says that things are as they are because Providence so wills, and there is nothing to be done about it. It is a fatalism which discourages effort and profitable thought.

Thyine Wood

BEFORE TOUCHING UPON THE PROPER PINES, THERE IS another member of the Cypress group which should be noticed, as it receives a passing mention in the Apocalypse under the name of *Thyine* Wood.

There seems to be no difference of opinion among commentators in designating as the tree intended one of the Thuyas, of which we possess familiar examples in our Arbor Vitæ, one species of which is native to New England, and others are imported and cultivated in gardens. The native tree *(Thuja Occidentalis)* is known as the White Cedar in Maine, and is valuable for its soft, fragrant wood, of light reddish-brown color, which is much used for shingles, and also for posts, being very durable.

The foliage of the cultivated trees is made close and thick by pruning, in which state they are planted for hedges, and pruned into quite solid walls and many fanciful shapes. The branches, with their many twigs clad in minute scale-like leaves, are flat; but the flat sprays do not lie horizontally like those of the cedar and the hemlock spruce; there is much variety in their direction, but, on the whole, they have a vertical tendency.

The "Thyine" wood Mr. Grindon describes as follows:

Being highly balsamic and odoriferous, it was used for incense in primeval religious ceremonies, and thence received its name of *thu-on*, or "wood-of-sacrifice," as instanced by Homer in his charming description of the enchanted island of Calypso (Od. V. 60). The tree which yields it is the *Thuja articulata* of *Desfontaines*, the *Callitris quadrivalvis* of Ventenat, and the "Algerian Cypress" of English catalogues. Nearly allied to the arbor vitæ, it presents itself as a branching evergreen, provided with innumerable slender twigs, which are curiously jointed, clothed with minute leaves, and decked, in their season, with a profusion of inconspicuous yellowish flowers. Upon all the wild and uncultivated hills of Barbary and Mount Atlas it is still to be found, though the majestic examples that grew anciently have seen no successors. The wood was valued not only for its odor when burned, but for its beautiful color—a dark and variegated hazel brown—and its smooth and solid texture. Under the name of citrus, citron, or citrine wood (just as we nowadays say "rosewood," the odor of the latter corresponding with that of the flower), it was employed for the highest and most costly descriptions of cabinet-work. Cicero, Martial, and Lucan refer to its splendor and value; while Theophrastus recommends that it should be employed in the building of temples, seeing that edifices dedicated to the deities should be constructed of imperishable materials, and that the callitris wood in particular is one that bids defiance to the hunger of insects.

The sacrifices of the ancients consisted chiefly of innocent animals, and represented the reception of good affections from God, and the acknowledgment of all goodness as His. The custom of offering fragrant resin and gum, and sweet wood, for sacrifice, had its origin in the days when the significance of all these things was understood; and they were employed with careful discrimination and exact intention. The wood, therefore, which preeminently was called the "wood-of-sacrifice," must preeminently represent the knowledge of the reception of good affections from God.

The distinct horizontal planes of the Cedar represent, as we have seen, a rational discrimination between the several planes of the human mind; but the vertical planes of the Thuya foliage, blended, as they are, without vertical stratification, represent a perception of the principle which unites all planes of the mind from inmost to outmost; and that principle is the love of God. From this point of view, therefore, we come to the same conclusion, that the tree represents a knowledge of the good affections received from God, and of their unity.

Thyine wood is associated in the Bible with "vessels of ivory," and therefore is said by Swedenborg to represent the natural good correlative to the truth represented by ivory (*Apocalypse Revealed* §774). Now ivory represents the same as the teeth, which are the guards of the nutrition of the body; and that is, the principles of good life by which everything ought to be examined before it is admitted to the halls of the mind or of the community. The good correlative with such truth is the knowledge of the increase of life from the reception of such things as bear the test. It is the knowledge of the reception of life from God by those who pass the gates of heaven, and the consequent increase of the life of heaven; it is the knowledge of the increase of good affection in the Church by the presence of those who bring upright lives to her service; it is the knowledge of the gift of good affections from God to those who are in the effort to do right.

Pines

OF ALL THE CONIFERS, AND, INDEED, OF ALL TREES THAT grow, pines most abound in resin. It is not of so fragrant a kind as some of the Eastern aromatic resins, yet it is pleasant in odor, and healing, and, in the forms of tar and pitch, is extensively used to protect from the weather ships and cordage and houses. Indeed the idea of protection is associated with the pine in every shape. Pine forests are the best of natural shields against cold winds. Their leaves, falling in autumn, make an even winter blanket over the plants beneath, and over their own roots. Their wood is the best of all wood for boards and clapboards and shingles for the outsides of houses; and it is the most easily worked and extensively used for doors, casings, and inside finish generally, and for drawers, cupboards, and tables. The pitch pine of the South makes enduring floors, and its resinous sap, as has been said, is protection itself against rain and water.

It should not be overlooked that the seeds of some pines, as the stone pine of Europe, and the sugar pine of the Pacific slope, are edible, and are an important article of food to the native inhabitants of their respective countries.

Pines, and also spruces and firs, send off their principal branches at regular intervals, separated by a year's growth of the leading shoot; and, therefore, have a tendency to stratification. Old pines generally lose their lower branches, and expand the upper branches in a broad head, which is especially marked in the stone pine, giving it the name of the "parasol tree." An old white pine, by losing branches at intervals, frequently shows two or three widely separated ragged floors of verdure. The pines naturally inhabit temperate or cool climates, and will thrive in sandy soil too poor to support other large trees.

The resinous quality of the pine shows that it represents a knowledge which appeals to the affections; the abundance of its inflammable sap indicates the fiery thought with which that knowledge is cherished; and the uses to which it is put show that the loved principles relate to the protection of men in the secure enjoyment of their homes, their possessions, their habits, and opinions; all these they protect from the cold of indifference, and the rain or flood of intrusive or violent instruction.

The pines, therefore, represent the principles of personal independence and the right of seclusion, in regard to natural, mental, and spiritual possessions. They are principles which, among Northern nations at least, are of all principles most vehemently defended. They are the principles which brought our forefathers across the ocean to enjoy the freedom of the New England forests; and which they expressed, more exactly than they intended, by stamping the figure of a pine tree upon their first-coined shillings. Probably a like association, with only a dim perception of its meaning, made a pine tree the banner of a Scottish clan. The Greeks worshipped Poseidon, called by the Romans "Neptune," as the "ruler of the sea, and as the first to train and employ horses" (Murray, p. 62). His temple stood in a pine grove, upon the Isthmus of Corinth, and the prize of the Isthmian games, celebrated in his honor, was a wreath of pine; apparently as a sign of independence of thought.

There is an undeniable sense of gloom in pine woods, which characterizes also an excess of personal independence; and, on the other hand, there is a restfulness in their soli - tude, which represents the enjoyment of needful seclusion. As the resin of the sap, so inflammable and hot, represents the zeal which enters into the idea of independence, the sugar which often accompanies it represents the natural sweetness of the same. The edible seeds of some species represent the *duty* of attaining and securing some kinds of independence. But as this is a serious duty only in relation to matters of conscience and religion, a few of the nobler pines only have seeds which are of any importance as food. The habit of the pines of dropping their lower branches as they grow older, and, except in a few poorer species, never sending up new shoots from the stump, represents the usual decrease of care for matters of external independence as we mature, and the transfer of the sensitiveness to matters of conscience and of interior life.

That the wood of the tree with such a representation should be easily wrought into boxes, doors, clapboards, shingles, and many forms of protection and seclusion, seems perfectly natural.

The name "pine," as it occurs in our English Bible, is probably a mistranslation, and the pine does not seem to be really mentioned in the Word, unless it is included in the most general sense of the cedar; which is not unlikely, as it is a conspicuous evergreen upon Mount Lebanon, and is nearly akin to the cedar both spiritually and naturally.

Firs and Spruces

THE FIRS AND SPRUCES CONSTITUTING THE FAMILY *ABIES* differ from the pines in shape, and in the quality of the wood. They are more sharply conical than pines, having less lateral extension, and more prominent leading shoots. The stratification is very regular from the top to the bottom of the trees, though when they grow together in the forests, they lose their lower branches.

Their wood is resinous, but much less so than pine. It is harder, and not so easily worked; but, on account of the straightness of its stems, it is especially valuable for frames of buildings where its size is sufficient; it is also sawed into boards for outside covering and flooring.

It grows with the pine, but also in colder climates, extending up the mountainsides, almost, or quite, to the limit of the growth of trees.

The regular pyramidal form of these trees, with their prominent leading shoot, and marked stratification throughout, suggests the principle of orderly subordination in the mind, in the family, in Church and State, and in the heavens, as their correlative.

In this view, a knowledge of what is proper to each plane of the mind, or of life, and its relation to others, constitutes, successively, the several strata of branches; and the leading shoot is the effort to attain the knowledge of the leading principle, the ruling love, or the head. Some intermediate twigs or small branches usually grow between the layers, like common ground between different planes of life. These are rare and very small between the nodes of the pines; for the spirit of independence prefers to keep its place even more strictly than rules of order require.

The trees naturally grow together, and they work well together in building also; for the principles of order very properly constitute the frame, the coarser boarding, and the common floor, which give general shape to the family life, while the details are finished with knowledge of individual rights and privileges.

That the principle of subordination survives in states too intensely cold and discouraging for the spirit of independence, is evident from the history of despotisms.

Review of Cone-Bearing Trees

UPON REVIEWING THE FAMILY OF CONE-BEARING TREES, it will appear, I think, that they all have relation to the organic life of the human race. The cedar illustrates the degrees of human life from outmost to inmost; the sequoia, the unity of the churches and races; the cypress shows that the race lives on forever with God in heaven; the juniper, that the same God is with us upon the earth, making angels of men; and the thuya, that the Lord's love permeates the whole, blessing every effort to do right. The pines maintain the right of liberty to individuals and societies; and the spruces and firs, the necessity for good order and subordination.

All these trees are resinous, because their spiritual correlatives are essential to happy life. They are loved, not merely because they are beautiful and true, but with something of the zeal and fire of the love of life. They are also evergreen, because the perceptions which their leaves represent cannot do their work, and then intermit; but must be ever active. Some of the fruit trees relate to useful work which may be done, and then a rest; some timber trees also relate to kinds of knowledge that grow as they have opportunity, and rest between whiles. But not so the trees which represent a knowledge of principles essential to everyday life; these may, indeed, have seasons of special growth, but their activity cannot be wholly suspended even for a day.

The fruits of these trees are cones. The seeds are not shut up in close seed vessels, but lie open upon the scales, which are arranged in beautiful spirals. In pines and spruces, the cones are sometimes very large, and contain many seeds; in other trees, they are smaller; and in the cypress and juniper the fleshy scales consolidate into little berries containing very few seeds each, but the berries are numerous. The pollen-bearing cones are distinct from the seed-bearing—sometimes on separate trees.

Several of these facts are to be explained by the relation of the trees to organized social life. The spiral cone, with its many scales, represents one's idea of a community, as to the good qualities of companionship, neighborhood, separate independence, and beautiful order. The seeds nestled at the base of the scales represent the principles of life of the community, which, in the case of the edible pine seeds, are also duties. That they lie open upon the scales—not shut up in a seed vessel or fruit—is because they represent the public laws of society, and not merely the results of individual experience. The fertilization of the seeds by flowers in separate clusters, and sometimes on separate trees, is because these principles are not developed in solitude; they are principles of social life, and are developed by association. How otherwise could the first suggestions of the laws of social order, of degrees in human life, of the unity of mankind, and even of the necessity for independence be received? If received at all, it is manifest that they would be much less abundant and perfect in solitude than in a community; and this is true, also, of ideas of immortality, of the Divine Providence with men, and of the blessing of God upon a good life.

The cones of the cypress and juniper are small and fleshy, like berries, because our real knowledge of the providence of the Lord, in relation to this life and the other, is derived from personal experience within a small circle, and is a matter of gratitude and affection, as well as of knowledge.

THE SHITTAH TREE

MR. GRINDON SAYS, IN AGREEMENT WITH THE *DICTIONary of the Bible:*

> It has long been known that by *shittah* is intended
> one of the species of the beautiful genus acacia, the
> Hebrew word being no other than the Egyptian
> *sont*, or *sunt*, by which name it is known to the pres-
> ent day in the ancient country of the Pharaohs, the
> *n* being omitted when the word passed into the
> language of the Old Testament.

Dean Stanley also remarks, in speaking of the vegeta-
tion of Sinai:

> The wild acacia, under the name of *sont*, every -
> where represents the *seneh*, or *senna*, of the Burn -
> ing Bush. A slightly different form of the tree,
> equally common under the name of *sayal*, is the
> ancient *shittah*, or, as more usually expressed in the
> plural form (from the tangled thickets into which
> its stem expands), the *shittim*, of which the taber -
> nacle was made—an incidental proof, it may be
> observed, of the antiquity of the institution, inas-
> much as the acacia, though the chief growth of the
> desert, is very rare in Palestine.

The name acacia means the thorn tree, and no name could be better deserved; for not only are the trunk and branches beset with pairs of thorns, but every twig presents a thorny point. And yet it is a pretty tree; the foliage with its many leaflets is graceful, and in the spring the tree is illumined by innumerable little golden balls of fragrant blossoms.

It is abundant everywhere in Egypt and in the desert, and furnishes the natives with the toughest material for tools and the frames of their boats, a considerable part of their fuel, and the gum arabic of commerce. The wood is close-grained, heavy, and extremely enduring; some specimens still exist which are believed to be five or six thousand years old.

Fruit trees correspond to intelligence concerning good uses, and their twigs are the particulars of such intelligence. But some fruit trees, when growing wild or neglected, harden their twigs into thorns, as is the case with pear trees; and such twigs correspond to intelligence, not about uses to others, but about protection from intruders. However unsatisfactory in a character it may be to find only reserve and caution against intrusion, where we have a right to expect open-hearted friendliness, yet there is a right place and a use for such protection. Such an attitude of mind is necessary towards the idle and wasteful, and still more towards those who come with worse intent. There is a use in walls and gates to the Holy City, to protect the inhabitants by shutting out evil; and the natural walls of the vegetable kingdom are thorny shrubs and trees.

The noblest plants of this class are the acacias; and the noblest corresponding spiritual growths are those of a knowledge of the Divine protection—a knowledge which comes from experience of the Divine power in repelling and shutting out evil from the mind. Swedenborg says that *shittim* wood "denotes the good of merit and of justice, which is of the Lord alone. The reason why it also denotes love is because the Lord, when He was in the world, from Divine love fought against all the hells and subdued them, and thereby saved the human race, and hence alone had merit, and was made justice; wherefore the good of the Lord's merit is His Divine love" (*Arcana Coelestia* §10178). That is to say, this wood corresponds, in individuals and in the heavens, to the sense that the Lord alone fights for man against the hells, and to the consequent sense that His is all the power of good. The same thing is taught in other passages, especially in *Arcana Coelestia* §9486, 9715; in the latter of which numbers, after repeating that shittim wood denotes "the good of merit and justice which are of the Lord alone," these terms are explained as follows:

> By His merit is meant that He fought alone with all the hells, and subdued them, and so reduced into order all things in the hells, and then at the same time all things in the heavens. . . . The good of the Lord's merit is also now the continual subjugation of the hells, and so the protection of the faithful; this good is the good of the Lord's love, for, from Divine love in the world, He fought and conquered. From Divine power thence acquired in the human, He afterwards alone fights and conquers to eternity for heaven and for the Church, thus for the universal human race, and thereby saves them. This now is the good of merit, which is called justice, because it is of justice to restrain the hells which endeavor to destroy the human race, and to protect and save the good and the faithful.

The planks of the tabernacle were of *shittim* wood, representing the sense, in heaven and in the Church, of the sustaining and protecting power of the Lord's love (*Arcana Coelestia* §9634). The ark also, and the table, and the altars were of shittim wood, overlaid with gold or with brass; because the acts and states of worship which they represent are interiorly of the Lord's saving power.

Swedenborg, in *Arcana Coelestia* §9472, speaks of the *shittim* wood as a "species of cedar," following Schmidius in the comment which he several times intrudes into his text, and into his translation of Isaiah 41:19. But that light of heaven which does reveal heavenly things, though not natural, caused Swedenborg consistently to see and to teach that everywhere the *shittim* wood stands in the Word for a knowledge of the saving and sustaining power of the Lord, and not for the rational knowledge of the relation between things natural and spiritual, which, as he uniformly states, is represented by the successive planes of verdure of the cedar tree.

It is interesting to notice that the acacia is a tree of the desert, or of the borders of the desert, as the knowledge of the Divine protection is a knowledge that grows in states of temptation. The beautiful foliage of many leaflets, twice compounded, in some related species sensitively shrinking from the lightest touch, are the tender reachings out for a perception of the Divine protection from the many evils that beset us, in general and in particular. The golden balls of fragrant flowers are the joy of perceiving and confessing that the Lord is good, though we are not, and that in Him we are safe. The pure adhesive sap may be the thought from such perception that all good things are from Him, and therefore are one.

WILLOWS AND POPLARS

I<small>T IS DIFFICULT TO BE SURE OF THE TREES INDICATED BY</small> these names in the Bible. Probably the Hebrew terms for both are somewhat more comprehensive than our English words, and include a variety of stream-loving trees and shrubs. The Hebrew names for the poplars and the willows seem to be derived from *whiteness*, and many species of both are silvery in appearance, especially when the leaves are blown up by the wind. Willows are fond of the "water courses"; and Lombardy poplars, and also the similar species which is abundant in northern Palestine, are no less so. In moist places, they both grow with great rapidity; and their slender, flexible twigs are everywhere used for basket work. Poplar stems of larger size, from their lightness and straightness, are a favorite wood for rafters. Both trees have their flowers in catkins, the stamens and the pistils on separate trees, and produce a profusion of small, cottony seeds, which blow like down in the wind. The long, slender leaves, which are common among willows, bear a strong resemblance to olive leaves, and some of the large trees are strikingly like olives in general appearance. And, on the other hand, the Lombardy poplars, with every shoot pointing upward as straight as possible, equally resemble the cypress in general appearance. It is also worthy of mention that several of the poplars, by reason of their flattened leaf stems and quivering leaves, are universally taken as symbols of fearfulness and tremulousness.

Swedenborg assigns to both the representation of a low order of intelligence, relating to "natural good" (*Arcana Coelestia* §4013), and the "lowest goods and truths of the natural man, which belong to the external sensuals" (*Apocalypse Explained* §458).

As the cypress, with its evergreen ascending twigs, corresponds to a knowledge of eternal life in heaven, the poplar—which is so similar in form, but with deciduous fluttering foliage—seems to represent a knowledge of spiritual influences in the natural world—an external sensual knowledge, as of spirits and ghosts, and their influence upon the affairs of men, which, because of its lack of spiritual intelligence, is subject to superstitious fears and fancies.

The willows, in their resemblance to olive trees, represent a similar knowledge of dependence upon the Lord in regard to natural things—such, for instance, as the Israel - ites had when they heard from their fathers what works were done by the Lord in the days of old, such as is given in the literal story of the Scriptures, and such as is prominent in our national Thanksgivings. Neither tree bears serviceable fruit, but they fill the air with their downy seeds. And so do the simple with their whispers of spirits and ghosts, on the one hand, and, on the other, with sentiments of dependence, which with many take the form of belief in charms and omens, or better, in faithful observance of religious forms. The pliable character of this intelligence, relating to external good from a spiritual or Divine origin, may be the reason why the twigs of the trees so readily permit themselves to be woven into baskets for the reception of material goods. In this shape they represent a state of grateful reception and acknowledgment.

In the Scriptures, willows are associated both with rejoicing and with weeping: with rejoicing in times of prosperity and abundance; with weeping in times of captivity and scarcity. In the celebration of the Feast of Tabernacles, the Israelites were commanded to take, with other emblems, "willows of the brook, and rejoice before Jehovah seven days" (Leviticus 23:40). It is said also in Isaiah: "I will pour My Spirit upon thy seed, and My blessing upon thine offspring; and they shall spring up as among the grass, as willows by the watercourses" (Isaiah 44:4). In both instances they are spoken of as representatives of grateful rejoicing for benefits received. But in the Psalm (137:2), where it is said by the captives in Babylon, "We hanged our harps upon the willows in the midst thereof," they represent an acknowledgment of natural benefits from the Lord, given now to their enemies, and withheld from themselves. The pendulous boughs of some willows have been taken as forms of grief. And probably they do represent a clinging to the things of earth, and grief for the loss of them.

Shrubs and Flowers

In our study of trees, we have seen that the fruit trees represent wisdom of life of many useful kinds—concerning the Lord, the Church, marriage, social relations, benevolences, the care and education of children. The leaves of the trees represent perceptions of new truth; and the blossoms, all the parts of which are leaves modified by the expectation of fruit, represent the joyous perceptions of the application of wisdom to use.

The flowering shrubs are many of them akin to the fruit trees, but lack their stately size, and their nutritious fruitfulness. They are content with beauty and fragrance, without more substantial fruits; or their fruits are only berries. In this they represent intelligence concerning various affections, which is enjoyed as a good in itself. It is intelligence rather about being good than about doing good; or if it does other good works, they are pleasant and kindly rather than substantial.

A large part of the intelligence in children's minds is of this kind. They have not the mature reason to think out useful plans of life, or even to follow the details of such plans. But they love stories, especially such as illustrate clearly the good and the evil in human life. For such things their perceptions are quick. They are fond also of plays which imitate the works of maturer life—without their fullness of detail, but with a keen sense of their heroism, their self-sacrifice, their humility, their patience, and other virtues. This intelligence in virtue, if of a permanent kind, and with some development with years, agrees well with the nature of the flowering or fragrant shrubs. The annual flowers, herbaceous and short lived, are like the oft-recurring promptings to be good, to be gentle, modest, patient, hopeful, cheerful, grateful, and so on in a long series, when the admonitions are heeded in a spirit of obedience to the Lord, or to the Lord's representatives. It is not difficult to see in violets the beauty of a retiring modesty; in daisies, of humble cheerfulness; in lilies, of a more stately and serene hopefulness. The perception of such characteristics, as presented in the flowers, has always been an element in the art of the poets.

Our Lord in speaking of "the lilies of the field," probably did not refer to lilies in particular, for these are not conspicuous in Palestine; but used the term in a general sense for the flowers of the field. Beautiful flowers abound all over the land; and neither in color, in form, nor in texture, can any royal robes compare with them. This is not less true spiritually than naturally; for the flowers of the mind are spontaneous expressions of good feeling, and no elaborate array of artificial sentiment can compare in beauty with such as is spontaneous and genuine, and has in it life from the Lord.

Roses

OF ALL THE FLOWERING SHRUBS, PERHAPS ROSES PRESENT the greatest variety in form, color, and fragrance. Certainly they are unrivaled in the generosity of their blossoming, considering the size, fullness, abundance, durability, and succession of their flowers. They are akin to the great family of fruits that represent the wisdom of social life—the apples, pears, quinces, cherries, plums, peaches, and almonds. And the rose bushes themselves varying in size from a little bush almost to a tree and bearing flowers sweetly simple, or full almost as a cabbage—white, blushing pink, deep crimson, and even yellow—offer variety sufficient to cover a wide range of friendliness.

Swedenborg describes "rosaries" in heaven—one magnificent one arranged like a rainbow, within which sat the angel wives who instructed him in the wisdom of conjugial love (*Conjugial Love* §293, 294). The delights of such wisdom, they said, the rosaries represented; but from his mention of "roses or flowers," it appears that they did not consist of roses exclusively. Mr. Murray says that roses were strewn about Cupid, "to symbolize the sweetness and beauty of young love"; and that Hebe, the goddess of youth, was represented with a wreath of roses (*Mythology*, pp. 202, 208). The generosity and freshness of youthful friendship and admiration, in all their varieties of modesty and of exuberance, seem to be very fully represented by the roses.

The Box and the Myrtle

TWO EVERGREEN SHRUBS ARE THESE, HARDLY ATTAINING the size of trees, but valued as pretty ornaments of the garden. The wood of the box has always been a favorite for its close grain and golden color; and it is said that boxes were first made from it, and that the very name "box" is only the ancient name of the tree, "pyxos," slightly modified. Of boxwood, hitherto, the blocks for wood engraving have been made almost exclusively. The close foliage of the box has invited the shears of the gardeners, and caused it to be cut into borders and all manner of curious shapes, in all of which it retains a close, solid appearance.

The myrtle, besides its bright, clean foliage, is valued also for its fragrant white or rose-tinged flowers, and sweet-flavored berries.

Of myrtle bridal chaplets were made in old time, and also crowns for the victors in bloodless contests. The Muse of Love and Marriage Songs wore a wreath of myrtle and roses, which were also sacred to Venus.

The sweet-scented and ornamental shrubs represent a modest and pleasing intelligence, not intent upon important works, like that represented by the fruit trees, nor yet simply upon the acquisition of useful knowledge, like the spiritual timber trees; but content to apprehend intelligently, and present acceptably the virtues of life, as order, gratitude, humility, patience, friendship, and the like. Their very fragrance and beauty show that they represent some spiritual pleasantness or beauty; and the human qualities which are spiritually pleasant and beautiful are such virtues. The considerable size and longevity of the shrubs indicate a corresponding elevation and permanence of the correlative intelligence.

And among such varieties of intelligence, that concerning the value of order seems indicated by every characteristic of the box. The very name, and the fact of its long-recognized adaptation for the use which the name stands for, is an acknowledgment of the spirit that animates it; as is likewise its employment for borders in gardens. Its foliage—bright, clean, rigid, and evergreen—expresses as well as foliage can, the unremitting attention of such intelligence to details of neatness and propriety. The perfection with which it preserves the forms into which it has been cut indicates the same formal spirit; and it is a similar quality in the close-grained wood, which especially adapts it to engravers' purposes.

The more graceful and fragrant myrtle expresses a more graceful and pleasant intelligence than that of the box, more closely related to active affections. Its ancient employment for chaplets of brides, and its association with roses in the adornments of the Muse and the Goddess of Love, suggest the variety of intelligence represented; which must not be confounded with that of orange flowers, with their generous fruits of wisdom concerning marriage, but perhaps rather resembles the delicate beauty and less important fruitfulness of what Swedenborg calls "the chaste love of the sex," which is the introduction to marriage love, and afterwards its modest companion.

The myrtle is a sister to the pomegranate; and we have seen that pomegranates correspond to an abundant natural usefulness based upon Christian charity. The myrtle, more graceful and fragrant, though less showy in blossoms and fruit, must correspond to intelligence concerning some kind of affection, less practical, but more graceful and sweeter, and probably, as has been indicated, a pure affection between men and women. The love which we call "Platonic," which Plato understood as a love for beauty of mind, in either sex, indicative of intelligent receptiveness, and which delights in the stimulus of such beauty to intelligence and virtue, is not very far from the soul of the myrtle.

Thorns and Thistles

WE HAVE SEEN IN THE CHAPTER ON THE *SHITTAH* TREE that there is a kind of thorniness which designs no harm, but is intended for useful protection; which, in that instance, is borne by a tree both noble and graceful, and useful in many ways.

The thorns of roses, likewise, seem intended naturally for protection to the plant; and spiritually they appear to represent the caution, and even the jealousy, of friendship to prevent careless intrusion.

Besides the acacia there are very many thorny and prickly plants in Palestine. The nubk-apple is a small tree beset with strong thorns, and bearing small hard fruit, which the natives eat. There is a low, thick bush, spreading one to two feet, full of slender thorns an inch or two long; the camels gather it in with their leathery lips and horny tongue, and do not seem to be pricked in the least. There are thistles which in the plain of Gennesaret, and no doubt elsewhere, grow eight to ten feet high, and are so strong and sharp that horses cannot penetrate among them. There are nettles also which are not only sharp but stinging. These last, useless and almost maliciously hurtful in themselves, and preventing all useful productiveness, are certainly evil, and are like ill-natured minds, centered in self, and extending towards others only hard, repelling, censorious, and even malicious thoughts. When Adam and Eve were sent forth from the Garden of Eden, it was said that thenceforth the earth should produce for them thorns and thistles, representing the change in the state of mind from the bounteous kindliness produced while they were open to the Lord's love, to unfruitful censoriousness when they turned to self. A similar curse was pronounced upon the house of Israel by the prophet Isaiah: "Upon the land of my people shall come up thorns and briars" (Isaiah 32:13). And in Hosea it is said, "The thorn and the thistle shall come up on their altars" (Hosea 10:8). Our Lord spoke of seed sown among thorns, as the truth "choked by cares, and riches, and pleasures of this life"—the thorns standing for selfish and worldly intelligence in general, which is intent upon exclusive advantages to self.

Aromatics

THE THOUGHT OF EVERY MAN FROM HIS AFFECTION, whether good or bad, has an influence upon those whom he meets: it proceeds from him as an activity of his life around him. Many persons are very sensitive to these spheres of life; and all are more or less encouraged or depressed or in some way affected by them. In the spiritual world these spheres of life are sometimes perceived as odors; those of kind, friendly life as odors of flowers and fruits; and those of selfish, evil life as poisonous and putrid odors. The fragrant flowers and shrubs, which produce no fruit for food, but only diffuse sweetness and pleasantness around them, are like affections of friendship and gratitude, the very expression of which is pleasant and cheering, though they do no more substantial work. The stimulus to smell and taste imparted by spices represents the encouraging influence of such affections; and the noblest of the spices represent the noblest affections, which are those of gratitude and humility to the Lord, and affection for His good gifts of love and wisdom.

Aromatic Trees and Shrubs

OF AROMATIC TREES AND SHRUBS PERHAPS THE NOBLEST family is that of the Laurels, to which belong, besides the classic laurel, cinnamon trees and probably the ancient cassia, also camphor and sassafras and many other less familiar aromatics. Mr. Grindon says of cinnamon:

> The tree yielding it forms a beautiful laurel-like evergreen; the leaves are oval, somewhat acute, several inches in length, entire, and of a peculiar glaucous color; the little grayish-white flowers are produced in thin panicles.... In our own day the word Cassia has become the name of a Chinese spice bark resembling cinnamon, but somewhat coarser.

In the Bible, Cassia stands for a more precious aromatic than Cinnamon, possibly reversing the modern English application of the names.

In Grecian mythology, Polyhymnia, the Muse of Song and of Oratory, and Kalliope, the Muse of Heroic Poems, wore crowns of Laurel. The Laurel also was the prize of the Pythian games in honor of Apollo.

From this tradition successful poets in our time are said to wear laurels, and the leading poet of England is the Poet Laureate. The trees that bear sweet spices naturally represent the intelligence that perceives and stores up the sweet aroma of human experiences, that interprets their essence. This is true of all fragrant and resinous trees and shrubs in their degree, from the humblest to the noblest; they all represent the intelligence of some joys of life, homely or exalted. The understanding of the joys arising from the nobler motives and inspirations seems to be represented by Laurels.

In the Israelite ceremonial cinnamon and cassia were elements of the anointing oil by which the tabernacle and its furniture were sanctified, also with which the priests themselves were anointed that they might minister in the sacred things of the priests' office. This sanctifying oil represented the Divine influence in the Church; for this alone gives holiness to the Church. The olive oil which was the basis of it represents the general reception of the goodness of the Lord; and the spices with which it was compounded represent intelligence in regard to its benefits in the various planes of life, from the pleasures of sense to the inmost perceptions of the joy of life according to the Lord's commandments. The ascending series in which these degrees of intelligence are represented is "myrrh, cinnamon, sweet cane, and cassia," the cassia standing for the noblest of the series. Of Myrrh, Mr. Grindon says:

> The tree itself is described as one of low stature and rugged aspect; the branches thorny, and beset with small trifoliate, sessile, and bright green leaves; while the flowers are insignificant and clustered, and the smooth brown fruits somewhat larger than peas. The wood and bark emit a powerful odor; the gum, which exudes like that of cherry trees, but chiefly near the root, is oily at first, but hardens upon exposure to the air.

Such is the modest tree which stands lowest in the series, and therefore represents the sense of the Divine goodness in external things, as in the fruits of the earth and the things that contribute to natural comfort and protection. Its low stature, rugged thorny branches, and oily fragrant gum, all accord with this representation.

As these four aromatics represent intelligence concerning the goodness of the Lord in an ascending series, and myrrh represents such intelligence concerning sensual good, cinnamon relates to a sense of the Lord's goodness in natural orderly life, sweet cane to the same in a life of spiritual charity, and cassia to the inmost sense of the goodness of the Lord's love for men. The angels' sense of the goodness of the Lord in every degree is glad and grateful, and therefore is perceived as fragrant. Perhaps it is from this cause that when those angels of the celestial kind whose duty it is to attend upon the dead come near, the odor of death is perceived as aromatic. For death is of the Lord's love for raising men into heaven, and these angels perceive it so, and also the intensity of the Divine love that is there present.

> Something balsamic is perceived from dead bodies when the Lord is present, and celestial angels; and it was said that the Lord is especially present there, wherefore also celestial angels are there; because without such presence of the Lord, there would be no resurrection of the dead. (*Spiritual Diary Minor* §4702)

Another series of fragrant materials entered into the composition of the incense which was burned on the golden altar in the Tabernacle; and these are called in our version, "stacte, and onycha, and galbanum, these sweet spices with pure frankincense." The most important of these, frankincense, is thus described by Mr. Grindon:

> The substance in Scripture called lebonah . . . and in the authorized version, "frankincense," is a dry, brittle, glittering, and aromatic gum resin of bitter taste, the same that in nineteenth-century shops is called olibanum. Anciently it was used in sacri-

ficial fumigations, the freedom with which the fragrant vapor is diffused, while the clear and steady flame itself is not easily extinguished, rendering it specially suitable for such purposes. . . . The tree which produces olibanum . . . in stature is lofty; the foliage, which is deciduous, resembles that of the sumac, but is crowded at the extremities of the branchlets; the flowers are pink and star-shaped, half an inch or more in diameter, and are borne in erect and simple racemes rather shorter than the leaves. When the bark is wounded the frankincense flows out, delightfully fragrant, and dried by the atmosphere, presently hardens.

It is scarcely necessary to point out that the incense offered in the Jewish Church was a representative of the heartfelt and intelligent worship of the Christian Church. "Let my prayer be set forth before thee as incense, and the lifting up of my hands as the evening sacrifice," expresses the evident truth that the offering of incense and sacrifices was representative of true spiritual worship. The smoke of fragrant gums is not worship; but the ascent of fragrant human thought to the Lord is worship. And that human thought is fragrant to Him which is full of the sweetness of love. Nothing can make it fragrant but love; and the sweetness is according to the quality of the love. And the love must be not an intellectual sentiment of the moment, but founded in the life. "If thou bring thy gift to the altar, and there rememberest that thy brother hath aught against thee, leave there thy gift before the altar, and go thy way; first be reconciled to thy brother, and then come and offer thy gift." More than by any other manifestation, the inward goodness or badness of a thing is perceived by the scent; and no prayers are sweet-scented to the Lord which are not from sincere love and charity in the life. The tall tree bursting with fragrant gum, with leaves crowded to the ends of the branchlets as if at the finger ends of outstretched hands, is a representative of intelligent worship from such love.

The frankincense tree is related to the humble myrrh tree; and their fragrant gums, together with gold, constituted the offerings of the wise men to the infant Lord. It will be seen in its proper place that gold is a representative of experience of the love of the Lord in a life according to His commandments, which is full practical knowledge of His living presence. Frankincense is the representative of worship of the Lord from a life of charity; and myrrh, of acknowledgment of the Divine goodness in external comforts and pleasures. These were brought to the Lord in confession that the life of the Church in every degree is from Him; that He is God-with-us; and that worship internal and external belongs to Him alone.

Onycha

AMONG THE MATERIALS OF WHICH THE SWEET INCENSE was made was "onycha," which is believed to be a sweet-scented shell. The shellfish seem to be representatives of the love of protection and repose; and their shells, of the truth which gives such protection. The fragrant shell used in the incense may represent the grateful pleasure in the acknowledgment of this protecting truth; which is one appropriate element in spiritual worship.

Hyssop

A LOWER ORDER OF AROMATIC PLANTS WE FIND IN THE large family of mints. They are herbs or small shrubs, many of them pleasantly stimulating as perfumes, and some also as flavors for food or medicine. Among them we find lavender, thyme, sage, pennyroyal, savory, horehound, spearmint, and peppermint. Not one seems to be harmful, though there are some coarser kinds that are not specially valuable. Peppermint is perhaps the most extensively used, chiefly as a flavor, and with confectionery. It is an old remedy for simple colic, and in sensitive persons produces colic. The abundance of such plants in Palestine makes the whole air fragrant and delightful to breathe, when they give out their perfume in the dewy evenings. They are all square-stemmed, with irregular flowers producing each four little nutlets for seeds.

Such plants cannot represent a very exalted wisdom; but a very sweet, humble, domestic wisdom they certainly do represent to us. The squareness of the stems and the fruit suggests as their animating principle a love of spiritual squareness—of considering fairly all sides, and making sure of what is both right and wise. It is a modest wisdom, applicable to a great variety of subjects, springing up afresh for every occasion, and in general discerning what is wholesome, fit, and thoroughly good. With an uncon - scious sense of this meaning, mints are used to garnish dishes, to perfume the clean linen, to adorn cottage dooryards and gardens. Their pleasant, homely fragrance is a grateful expression of the satisfaction in fitness and whole - someness.

It is probable that the hyssop of the Bible, like the modern hyssop, was a mint, growing in little bunches from the cracks in old walls; and that these little bunches made natural brushes for sprinkling the blood of the sacrifices upon the altar, and the water of purification upon the tent and furniture of the dead. It has been supposed that the "cedar wood, scarlet, and hyssop," commanded in Leviticus 14:4, were arranged as a brush with a handle; and Miss Callcott suggests that such was the arrangement of the hyssop, called by Matthew and Mark "a reed," upon which the sponge of vinegar was offered to the Lord. She adds: "To this day the long haired brush used in Roman Catholic churches for aspersing with holy water, is called in many places the hyssop."

A sense of what is both good and right, or thoroughly wholesome and useful, discerns also why the contrary things are not good, and wherein they must be corrected or removed. A plant representing such a sense would, therefore, appear to be an appropriate instrument for the application of the water or the blood of purification, to represent the removal of what is unwholesome or unclean.

Mustard

SCARCELY AN AROMATIC, AND YET A CONDIMENT, THE MUSTARD may with some propriety claim a few words here. The least of the seeds sown in the garden, it yet may become the tallest of the herbs. In the plain of Buttauf, in the central part of Galilee, during the month of April, we rode among mustard plants ten and twelve feet high. Slender trees they were, with scant foliage; and yet they were specimens of very rapid herbaceous growth, tree-like in form. They belong to the family which gives us the water cress, cabbage and cauliflower, turnips, radishes, and horserad-ish—plants in which the roots, stalks, and leaves are the edible portions, and not the fruits. These food storers are mostly biennials, which devote the first year of their exis-tence to the gathering of material into themselves which they would expend upon the production of seed the sec-ond year. But the gathered materials are the use they do, and the seeds are only suggestions for gathering more. In this they are like men who spend their lives in gathering stores of wealth, or learning, or muscle, without any ulte-rior object; the stores themselves being good to them, and their use to the community. In accumulations of this kind there is much self-confidence, and sense of personal impor-tance; and yet there may be a generous willingness that the stores should be of use to others.

The mustard, though a member of the family, is an annual, and does not gather stores in this way; but its rapid pushing itself into the semblance of a tree, displays the same spirit of self-confidence and importance. Its chief use is in the seeds, which are sufficiently pungent to cause blisters when applied to the skin, or to be an active irri-tant in the stomach.

It may seem strange that the Lord should choose this as an emblem of faith, or of the kingdom of heaven; but it is an emblem only of the least of faith and the begin-ning of the kingdom of heaven. "A grain of mustard seed," Swedenborg says, "is man's good before he becomes spir-itual, which is the least of all seeds, because he thinks to do good of himself. What is of himself is nothing but evil; yet as he is in a state of regeneration, there is something of good, but it is the least of all things" (*Arcana Coelestia* §55). The faith which the disciples had—even James and John when they would have commanded fire to come down from heaven, and when they desired to sit, one on the right hand and one on the left, on the Lord's throne—had much self-confidence in it, and much expectation of being great and doing great things. In all this it was like the grains of mustard seed, aspiring and stimulating, but innocent and intending only good, even if somewhat irritating to their companions; producing, in fact, the same effect as chafing.

CEREALS

FROM THE FRUIT TREES, PERENNIAL AND USUALLY MANY-branched, is derived an important part of human food—the part that is most stimulating, pleasant, and refreshing; but the part that is most substantial and satisfying is derived from the lowly cereals. These are of humble growth, mostly of a single stalk. They produce their fruit quickly, and immediately perish; and therefore must be continually resowed, that there may be a succession of harvests. Their fruit is at first milky, but quickly dries and hardens, and must be both ground into meal and cooked by fire to prepare it for food.

We have seen that the fruits of trees correspond to various kinds of useful and interesting intelligence communicated from one to another: that the fruit of the olive represents intelligence concerning the goodness of the Lord; of the vine, intelligence in the wisdom of Christian charity; of the fig, in kindly beneficence; and of other fruit trees, intelligence in various social virtues and relations. Communication of such intelligence in social life is stimulating, pleasant, and refreshing; but this does not constitute the main satisfaction of life. The chief satisfaction of every day comes from doing faithfully the work of the day—the daily duties into which everyone puts his chief strength, and his best thought for the good of others. And these are the cereals; quickly sown and ripened, and constantly sown again; dry and monotonous; and yet full of love of work, and of satisfaction in its goodness. The pleasantness of social communications is represented by the sweetness of fruits. But the pleasure of good work is hardened into a sense of satisfaction in its goodness, which is expressed by the starch of the grains; to which is added an abundance of the gluten, or muscle-making substance, which is manifestly the embodiment of the love of useful work. The sense of satisfaction in the goodness of one's work may easily become a pride in superior merit, and express itself in "starched" manners and apparel.

If we see useful works done, and are acquainted with the love and thought from which they are done, we may be strengthened and delighted by them without any further process of preparation; as the disciples following the Lord, listening to His words, and seeing His works, plucked the ripening ears of wheat as they walked, "and did eat, rubbing them in their hands" (Luke 6:1). Or even while we see them we may be fired with a desire to do such works ourselves; which is like roasting the green ears, and eating them, as is frequently done in Palestine and in the Bible story.

But as soon as the grain is dry, to prepare it for food we grind it between millstones, knead the flour with water, and bake it before the fire. And by a corresponding pro - cess we get nourishing food from good works done no matter how long ago. In our effort to bring out their real interior quality, we assume a general basis of knowledge of circumstances, which we place like the lower millstone, and then with another inflexible stone of what it is natural to do under such circumstances, we examine the works, and compel them to yield their treasures of thought and feeling. Such treasures, to be food for us, must be mingled with the truth of what is adapted to us and to our uses, which is spiritual water, made as it were into cakes or loaves sufficient for our need, and, by the delight of love, compacted as in a new fruit of the wisdom of usefulness. Then we can receive it into our own thought, intention, and life, and make it a part of our souls.

We may also be nourished, not by others' harvests, but by our own. For, in doing our duties, there is an increase of wisdom and love of use, which themselves are food to the spirit. By such food are the interiors of angels' minds nourished; and when they come out into more external states, after their labor, their tables are spread with the bread, the wine, and the fruits, which correspond to the love and wisdom received interiorly.

The duties of everyday life are not all done from affection or principles of the same kind. Many persons—a great many at the present day—work because they are compelled to work for the support of themselves and their fam - ilies; many also work from love for an industrious, useful life; some because they see benefits which they sincerely desire the community to enjoy; and some because their Lord worked and still works; and in a useful life, according to His instructions, they can be with Him. And, as it is the spiritual principle within the work which corresponds with the harvest, not the particular trade or other outward form of employment, according to the kinds of these principles are the general kinds of grains.

Wheat

THE MOST NUTRITIOUS AND WHOLESOME OF ALL THE grains is wheat. It has been used from the earliest times, and in all countries. In thoroughly tilled, rich soil, it yields abundantly; but in rough, stony, weedy land it produces almost nothing. Its seeds possess great vitality, and will germinate after many years, or after exposure to cold and wet that kills the other grains. So valuable is it as food for man, that it is rarely given to animals or distilled for drink. It is used generally in the form of bread; which is so much the most important article of food, that, in the Bible as well as in common speech, it stands for food of every kind.

The noblest of the grains must represent the principles of the noblest work—that is, work done from the Lord. The Lord's example in serving is our seed; the plan for doing like it is our plant; the Lord's love for the use, and His wise thought perceived in us, are the sap which deposits all its goodness in the fruit.

Of such goodness and such wisdom of use are made the bread which is the best of all nourishment for human souls. In the tabernacle of the congregation, upon the golden table before the face of the Lord, were set always cakes of bread made of fine wheaten flour; because the Lord always gives to those who seek His face the support of His pure love of serving.

Therefore, when the Lord came into the world, and lived from that love Infinitely and Divinely in His own Humanity, bringing it forth clearly, that men might know it and receive it from Him, He said, "I am the living Bread that came down from heaven. If anyone eat of this bread, he shall live forever" (John 6:51). The same is meant also by the Bread of the Holy Supper—namely, the Lord's own love of doing good.

If we would have harvests of heavenly wheat, our hearts must be deeply, thoroughly tilled. No weeds of selfish thinking must be left, no stony objections, no obstinate indifference. We must be thoroughly yielding and willing, full of desire to do the Lord's will and nothing else. Such soil will do good works from the Lord plentifully. Their seeds will live in it, patiently awaiting their opportunity, through discouragements that would destroy less noble principles, and will bear fruit that may go on increasing forever in heaven.

Spelt

SPELT IS A SPECIES OF WHEAT WHICH WILL GROW UPON rougher land. It is distinguished from wheat chiefly by its closely investing wraps of chaff. In an ear of spelt each kernel is wrapped in two overlapping *paleæ*, and each cluster or spikelet of two to five kernels is held so firmly by a pair of stiff glumes that considerable force is required to liberate the grain. The stalk, or rachis, is so brittle that these spikelets easily break off, to the great inconvenience of the farmer. The correspondence of spelt would seem to be with works done for the Lord's sake, yet not so much in the freedom of His Spirit as in literal adherence to His teachings, which are loved for their own sake, and not merely to introduce good life. "The wheat and the spelt were not smitten" by the hail in Egypt; "for they were not grown up"; but "the flax and the barley were smitten." The wheat and the spelt Swedenborg here interprets as meaning the good of interior life and its truth, which are undeveloped in those here meant by the Egyptians; but the things of external religious life are practiced by them and can be destroyed.

Rye

BOTANICALLY AKIN TO WHEAT, AND NEXT TO IT AMONG the grains for nutriment, is Rye. Like wheat, it is used to make bread, but it is also distilled for intoxicating drink. Its heads are thinner than those of wheat, having only two rows and two flowers in the place of four; the individual grains, too, though of equal length with those of wheat, are less round and full. It excels the wheat only in the length of its straw. It will grow profitably, also, where wheat will not, on sandy soil, with little care.

That the grain is so similar to wheat, means that the works to which it corresponds are similar. They grow, however, from a mind less tender, less humble, and less full of desire for good. They are more elaborate in their theory, but less full in their accomplishment. They seem to be works that are done rather from love for the truth than for the goodness of the Lord; and to have more of the conceit of wisdom than the works represented by wheat; for these, more full of love, are also more humble and undemon - strative.

Barley

ANOTHER GRAIN, A LITTLE FURTHER REMOVED FROM WHEAT botanically, and still less nutritious than rye, is Barley. It is easily produced in every climate that is habitable by man, and in some countries is extensively used for bread for the poor. It is malted for beer, and is given for provender to horses and cattle.

The good which it represents, Swedenborg says, is exterior natural good, as that represented by wheat is interior natural. It is good that is pleasant to the natural, social, and animal affections. To be hospitable, and to make others comfortable and happy, in imitation of the Lord's works, but of ourselves, and without the interior humility which perceives the Lord's influence in the works, is to produce harvests of barley. It is the good that is most generally taught and practiced in the Christian world; for our Lord has not yet been fully known. The most precious good that He would give has not yet been widely received; but with five barley loaves have the whole Christian multitude been filled.

That rye and barley are so freely used in the preparation of intoxicating drink may be because principles of the kinds represented by them are stored in the mind, not for use, but to intoxicate him who possesses them. The whiskey made from rye seems to answer well to an intoxicating pride of wisdom; and the malt liquors made from barley to the mild intoxication of pride in good nature.

Oats

A VERY DIFFERENT GRAIN FROM THESE, ONE THAT IS NOT mentioned in the Word, is Oats. It is a grain that grows quickly in cold climates, is raised more easily than either wheat or rye, and is the favorite food of horses, for whose benefit it is generally cultivated. It is also eaten by invalids, and by some others, especially the Scotch, in whose country it attains the greatest perfection. Now horses represent, as has been shown, a love of understanding; and the Scotch are eminently an intellectual, reasoning people. And when one loves to reason, and see and explain why a thing should be done, then all the reasons for doing it, and doing it just so, invest everything he does, as the ample upper *palea* invests the oat. Such rational uses he will do, and do them conscientiously and abundantly, in states too cold and poor for gentler works of goodness.

Rice

THE GRAINS MOST COMMON AMONG US ARE NOT NECESsarily the food of all the world. The millions of people dwelling in India, China, and other parts of Asia use little of the food that is important to us, but subsist chiefly upon rice. We, too, use rice as a light, easily digestible food, mostly for children and invalids. Unlike wheat, which contains much of both starch and gluten, rice is composed mostly of starch, which alone is unsuitable for bread. It is therefore seldom ground, but is boiled whole, needing only to have its thick, innutritious hull removed.

The immense multitudes of people who live chiefly upon rice are all childlike. Industrious they are, but their industry is the simple industry of children. They do faithfully what they are told to do, copy minutely the patterns that are given them; they enjoy doing over and over again what they have been taught, but have no strength to originate or to overcome new difficulties. Their satisfaction is the satisfaction of faithful obedience to those whom they love and respect; and to the uses of obedience their rice corresponds. As the rice does not need to be ground, but easily softens by boiling, so neither does the affection of their works need laborious examination; it is simple homogeneous love of obedient serving. To get at the affection, however, we must separate it from the letter of the commands obeyed, which may be held tenaciously, but unintelligently, and which has no share of the kindly affection in it.

The fire by which food is prepared for use we have seen to be our own zealous love for duty or usefulness. Water is the truth of right and wrong. To heat the water is to combine our zeal with the truth which shows our duty. And to boil the rice is to reflect upon the uses of obedience given us to do, with the desire to do our duty rightly, till the innocent delight of them is open to us, and we can easily receive and appropriate it.

Maize

THERE REMAINS TO BE STUDIED INDIAN CORN, OR MAIZE; the cheapest and most abundantly produced of the grains; which furnishes food for cattle as well as for man; which flourishes upon the coarsest and grossest of manures, producing large, sweet stalks, and flowers with their parts not conjoined as in the other grains in their own little chambers, but separated, the stamens together in a showy tassel, and the pistils in a silky tuft projecting from the ear.

This least noble, but most abundant of the useful grains, suggests at once the most common and ignoble of the good motives for work—a desire to earn an honest living and the good things of the world.

Certainly works from this motive are done more for the animal than the spiritual part of man; they are stimulated by the coarsest examples and experiences of others; their plans may be large, showy, and pleasant to the natural mind; and there is in them no regard for the sweet satisfaction of the conjunction of every truth with its own goodness, but instead, a love of general approbation and admiration. There are varieties in such works corresponding to the varieties of the grain. Some are done reluctantly and scantily by persons who love their own ease, and work from necessity, to obtain the means of living and of indulgence. Some are done abundantly and well by persons who are eager to "get on" prosperously in the world. And some—the sweetest and softest of them all—are done from a desire to provide comfortably for one's family; and these, if done faithfully and honestly, have in them good human, though natural, affection.

Thus the Lord provides satisfaction for human souls in their daily work even from the lowest of harmless motives. But he offers to all the noblest of satisfactions. He brought down from heaven the purest delight in serving, from the Infinite Divine Love; and this He urges upon us all.

> Oh, that my people had hearkened unto me and Israel had walked in my ways! . . . He should have fed them with the finest of the wheat; and with honey out of the rock should I have satisfied thee. (Psalm 81:13, 16)

The Solanum Family

To the Solanum family belong the Potato and the Tomato, also a long list of narcotics, among them Tobacco, Belladonna, Hyoscyamus, and Stramonium. These plants have so important a place in modern life that it is worthwhile to give them some attention. They all have narcotic properties—even the potato leaves and seeds being poisonous. In general, they produce a soothing, stupefying, dreamy condition, in the extreme amounting to coma or paralysis; or, in the reaction, a state of irritability, wild excitement, and delirium.

The Mandrake

The only mention of this family in the Word appears to be that of the mandrakes which Reuben found in the field in the time of wheat harvest, and brought to his mother Leah. They are mentioned also in Solomon's song. The Mandrake is believed to be the same as the Mandragora, which is not uncommon in Palestine. It has a long, forked, fleshy root, with a bunch of leaves close to the ground— the flowers and fruit growing on slender stalks among the leaves. The flowers are said to be dingy white with purple veins, and the fruits pale orange, about the size of small crabapples. The fruit is regarded as possessing amatory powers, and is much esteemed by Orientals. Swedenborg speaks of it as used in Genesis to represent "the things of conjugial love" (*Arcana Coelestia* §3942; *Apocalypse Explained* §434), which is indicated also by its common reputation. No very elevated wisdom can be represented by such ground fruit, but rather the most external wisdom of love and its duties.

The Potato

POTATOES GROW UPON UNDERGROUND STEMS, AND ARE made up of buds with a deposit of starch to ensure their growth. The plants produce seeds, yet the chief means of propagation is the planting of the tubers; and these tubers are the useful, nutritious product of the plant. This seems to indicate a method of propagation in the works they represent, not so much by instruction, and the communication of principles, as by an unthinking initiation into habits of work and usefulness, as children are initiated at home, and others by companionship. Their growing underground indicates the entire lack of spiritual elevation and intelligence in such productions.

Starch, of which the potatoes are largely composed, is in itself a wholesome nutriment, and, as we have seen, has a correspondence with the satisfaction of good work— here it is the satisfaction of faithfulness to the interests into which one is initiated. Such blind initiation and faithfulness go together in very many of the modern combinations of society. Churches and political parties, clans and cliques, neighborhoods and nations, as well as families, all train the young to some extent in this way. They introduce them into their own ways of thinking and living, not as a matter of principle, but as a matter of association for common benefit. Some proportion of this blind allegiance enters into almost everyone's life, especially in children and the simpleminded; and faithfulness to it constitutes a part of his self-satisfaction. But potatoes are liable to rapid decay; and this is true also of the allegiance of the young and the simple, when more knowledge of the world is given them. The potato plant also has in it sufficient poison to produce stupidity or delirium; and there is a similar spiritual narcotic in a blind and exclusive devotion to one's family or party or clan.

Tomatoes

Tomatoes grow upon plants very like the Potato plants. They are the fruit and not an underground tuber, and are almost entitled to a rank among refreshing fruits, instead of among vegetables. Usually, however, they are cooked, and frequently are used as sauce for more substantial viands. They represent some external, natural wisdom; and their bright red color, as well as their family, indicates that it is wisdom of domestic affection. It is neither comprehensive nor spiritual in quality; but simply the bright sociability of natural affection, which helps to make home cheerful and harmonious.

Tobacco

Tobacco is not used for food, but the leaves themselves are smoked for the sake of the poison which they contain. The effect of smoking upon one who is wholly unaccustomed to it is to produce nausea and vomiting; but when he becomes somewhat accustomed to it the effect is at first soothing and tranquilizing, relieving anxiety and nervous strain. No doubt it was from this effect that the American Indians were in the habit of smoking it in their "peace pipes," as a sign that hostilities were laid aside and antagonistic feelings tranquilized. But the secondary effects of the smoking appear in increased irritability and unsteadiness of the nerves; which indeed by excessive use of tobacco frequently become paralyzed. How like all this is to the principle by which men in their various combinations for gain or for pleasure agree to shut their eyes to their differences, that they may pursue together their common end! At first the idea of thus combining makes them sick with disgust; but they go on and force themselves, and quiet their sensitiveness and even their consciences, and learn to enjoy an artificial, dreamy friendship, from which they are very unwilling to awake. But when the end is attained, and perhaps before, a reaction may come, and show itself in violent irritability and repulsion. If not thus, it may be that the sensitiveness to differences, even in matters of right and wrong, may be wholly destroyed, paralyzed by continual reasonings in behalf of the artificial harmony, breathed in by the thought as the smoke is inhaled by the lungs.[1] The continued use of tobacco has a decided tendency to deaden the moral sensitiveness.

Probably there is a right place for some such reasoning in the strain and confusion of social relations, and a corresponding place for the drug; but it is better to see clearly all matters of difference, especially in matters of right and

---

1. Compare *True Christian Religion* §159, 446.

wrong, to be willing to put away all the wrong in ourselves, and to be kind to others in their efforts; also to lay aside frankly, as of small account, things that are not matters of principle; and thus to secure harmony on an intelligent Christian basis. The immense increase of the use of the drug in our day—no doubt stimulated by the increasing complexity of social relations—seems to be a shirking of this duty; which, nevertheless, will have to be done sometime, perhaps under conditions in some respects more favorable, but in some more difficult. The state of our country in relation to slavery, for some years before the war, was much like that of a man under the influence of tobacco. The other narcotics belonging to the family seem all to have relation to the narrow and exclusive attachments, friendships, partisanships, which, from childhood, produce on the one hand much of illusion and inertia, and on the other excesses of irritability, passion, and violence.

Pulse

In Egypt and Palestine an important part of the food of the people is composed of beans and lentils, several kinds of which are extensively cultivated. One very common small lentil, which is made into a porridge, is still called by the same name as the staple of Jacob's pottage, for which Esau sold his birthright. The coarse bread of the country is crumbed or dipped into it—the pottage seldom if ever being eaten without it. And so we read that "Jacob gave Esau bread and pottage of lentils; and he did eat and drink" (Genesis 25:34).

In general the family is a family of vines—the beans climbing by winding the stalk about other objects, and the peas by tendrils which are modified leaflets. They are nutritious, possessing muscle-making elements like the grains; but their meal does not, like that of the grains, compact into bread. Probably it is on account of this last peculiarity that Swedenborg says they represent "a collection of ill-connected scientifics," or things learned; or "doctrinals not yet conjoined to good, thus a collection of them without order" (*Arcana Coelestia* §3316).

Again he says that lentils correspond to "the good of doctrinals"; and explains that one first learns doctrinals, or teachings of truth, and presently is affected by them, and this affection is the good of the teachings (*Apocalypse Explained* §3332).

In some respects the Pulse as articles of food are akin to the grains; they contain like them the nitrogenized or tissue-making element, and they are hard and dry, and can be kept any length of time. They are grouped with the grains as food for man, in Genesis; for they both are herbs yielding seed, which are given to man for meat. They are not, however, ground into meal, as are most of the grains, and will not compact into bread; but, like rice, are boiled until they are soft, or altogether crumble away. Their sustaining properties as food indicate a correspondence with some form of satisfaction in work done. Their want of cohesion or compactness indicates the want of cohering plan and resolution, and coincides with Swedenborg's clue of "ill-connected scientifics"—that is, things learned and done from instruction, and not from intelligent thought. They seem to differ from rice, in that the chief element in the correspondence of rice is the duty of obedience, and the satisfaction of faithfulness to this duty; but the Pulse relate rather to a desire to learn how to do uses, and the doing of them in a voluntary, imitative way, according to instruction. The eagerness of the plants to climb, their absolute dependence upon other objects for support, and their willingness to attach themselves to anything that will give the support, all indicate a state of initiation into the uses of life, as in youth. The beans, from their twining bodily around the means of support and elevation, seem to relate to the learning of things that are loved because they are good; and the peas, from their mode of climbing by modified leaflets, appear to relate to the learning of what seems to be true and right; for leaves represent perceptions, or reception by the understanding.

The Cucumbers and the Melons, and the Leeks and the Onions, and the Garlic

THOUGH MELONS ARE SWEET AND FRUITLIKE, THEY CONtain little nourishment, yielding little but sweetened water for refreshment. In cucumbers, the water is not sweetened, but perhaps is slightly mucilaginous. They both grow upon vines running upon the ground, or lifting themselves very slightly by tendrils; holding themselves among fruit trees like the serpents among animals. In Egypt they are planted in the mud or sand of the bed of the Nile, as the waters recede in early spring; and soon bring their fruits to maturity. The Israelites, weary of the manna from heaven, said, "We remember the fish which we did eat in Egypt for nothing; the cucumbers, and the melons, and the leeks, and the onions, and the garlic" (Numbers 11:5), "all of which," Swedenborg says, "signify such things as are of the lowest natural, that is, the sensual-corporeal man" (*Apocalypse Explained* §513).

The sensual-corporeal part of man is strictly that which hungers and thirsts, and is affected by the things which please the palate, the eyes, the ears, the smell, and the touch. The part of the mind that is affected by these things loves also to hear of them, and is affected by knowledge concerning them or agreeing with them. A good sensual-corporeal mind likes in the news of the day such things as relate to innocent pleasure, and such as give warning of evil; but the more common perverse form loves the things that minister to evil. The melons and cucumbers are watery, and medicinally produce colic, and other affections of the digestive organs; and therefore they appear to be related to the intellectual senses, through which the mind is instructed—the hearing and sight especially.

When Elisha was visiting the company of the prophets in Gilgal, "he said unto his servant, Set on the great pot, and seethe pottage for the sons of the prophets. And one went out into the field to gather herbs, and found a wild vine, and gathered thereof wild gourds his lap full, and came and shred them into the pottage; for they knew them not. So they poured out for the men to eat. And it came to pass as they were eating of the pottage, that they cried out, and said, O man of God, there is death in the pot. And they could not eat thereof" (2 Kings 4:38–40). The pottage represents such instruction as they loved in merely literal things; and the "wild gourds" from the vine (supposed to be the colocynth, or bitter cucumber) represents erroneous ideas from natural, untaught, and untrained thought. And the casting in of meal, by which Elisha cured the evil, represents the application to genuine usefulness, by which idle speculation is made harmless. At their best, however, such vines cannot represent anything better than a knowledge of orderly pleasures of sense, and especially of sight and hearing.

The onions and leeks and garlic are valuable for their bulbs, which are the thickened bases of the leaves, growing in the surface of the ground. They represent an intelligence of no greater elevation than the others, and of less scope. From their pungency, and their relation to diseases of the skin, it would appear that the sensual-corporeal subjects to which they are related are those of the sense of touch and taste, and in some degree of smell, which are the senses which especially affect the feelings, as the sight and hearing do the thoughts. The plants are biennials, and the edible bulbs are the deposits of the first year's accumulation at the base of the leaves, which would furnish materials for the flowers and seeds of the second year. The food thus obtained has relation to knowledge, in this case sensual knowledge, gathered not with an immediate view to use, but as a good in itself, for present pleasure.

GRASSES

THE GRAINS ARE ONLY THE NOBLER GRASSES, MATURING seeds which are useful for food. They are related to the humbler grasses comparatively as fruit trees are to their allied flowering shrubs. To the grasses we owe the summer beauty of our meadows and hillsides and lawns, and also the greater part of the food of the domestic animals. The green pastures in which the sheep lie down are pastures of grass and other flowering herbage, which are correspondences of the teachings by which the Lord feeds His flock.

The grains are correspondences of duties done from various good motives; and the grasses which are so like the grains, but are themselves food for the humbler animals, and do not develop large, nutritious seeds which shall be food for man, correspond to knowledge *about* the duties of life which the grains represent, yet not themselves teaching duties to be immediately done. The instruc - tion of children in the broader aspects of life, which they like to know about, and to imitate in many childish plays, but which do not yet present duties to them, is like the grass of the field. The mind is nourished by it before it is prepared for the full satisfactions of useful life from duty to the Lord or from duty to the neighbor. And so also are they who are preparing for the heavenly life nourished in the introductory states before they enter into that life.

They are instructed concerning it, while they are yet in their natural states; and love to learn about it, and perhaps to learn very much, before they undertake its duties. And such instruction of the natural man before the satisfactions of the real life are received is like the grass and herbage with which the good animals are nourished. For the good animals correspond to such innocent, natural feelings.

Swedenborg tells us that "when there is discourse in heaven concerning instruction and teaching from the Word, then in the world of spirits, where spiritual things appear naturally, meadows green with grass, herbage, and flowers are represented to the sight, and also flocks there; and this occurs with every variety according to the quality of the discourse in heaven concerning instruction and teaching" (*Arcana Coelestia* §5201). And, again, "to find pasture is to be taught, illustrated, and nourished in Divine truths" (*Apocalypse Revealed* §914). In *Apocalypse Explained* §507, it is said that the green grass signifies the "scientific truth . . . by which spiritual truth is confirmed, and which has life from spiritual good"; where by scientific truth is meant truth about good life and heaven and the Church, learned as a child learns it. The beauty of an innocent, childlike mind, full of images and hopes of heaven and heavenly life, by which the innocent, natural feelings are delighted and satisfied, is the beauty of spiritual pastures of grass and herbage, with the sheep and the lambs feeding in them.

Reeds and Rushes

Somewhat like grasses in general appearance, but usually growing rank, by the streams and in wet places, are the reeds and rushes of many kinds. Among the rushes, we will for the present purpose include the sedges. The Biblical term includes both; and here, where we are trying only for general ideas, only the general characteristics common to both will be mentioned.

They are too coarse for food for the domestic animals, but are sometimes used for bedding and litter for them. Before the introduction of woven carpets, rushes were strewn upon the floors even of palaces, to protect them from filth. There is even an indication that the outer court of the temple at Jerusalem, where they were selling oxen and sheep and doves, was thus strewn; for the expression for a "scourge of small cords," with which the Lord drove them all out of the temple, means primarily a scourge of twisted rushes. Scouring rushes were also used, and are still used in some places, for soap and sand.

Plants of this nature, and fit for such uses, cannot correspond to truth that teaches about heaven, or heavenly life, nor even to such as teaches about good uses in this life; but they may correspond to the teaching of decency and decorum, of what is fit and becoming, or unfit and not to be done. This is evidently the meaning of rushes upon the floor, to say that it should not be defiled; of rushes for litter and of scouring also, and of the scourge with which the Lord drove from the temple court those who were defiling it. In reformation this lowest use must first be done, and then it gives place to the teaching of positive good uses. The promise of "grass for reeds and rushes" relates to "the establishment of the Church by the Lord; and that then there will be knowledge by means of the Divine Truth natural to those who had before only sensual truth, is signified by grass for reeds and rushes. Grass signifies knowledge from a spiritual origin, or by which spiritual truth is confirmed; but reeds and rushes signify knowledge from a sensual origin, or by which the fallacies of the senses are confirmed. This knowledge, regarded in itself, is only the lowest of natural knowledge, called material and corporeal, in which there is little or nothing of life" (*Apocalypse Explained* §627). As we have been speaking of it above, it is such knowledge of the best kind, showing what is not fit and decent; but the standard of what is fit and decent may have its origin either in the eternal truth, or in the conventionalities of the time, which exalt many artificial and foolish things, and make wholesome and natural ways improper. The "dragons" are they who externally are in appearances of good, but internally wicked. They lie and are at rest among those who judge only by appearances, and by a literal compliance with the precepts of the Word, though its spirit is wholly disregarded.

The Papyrus

THE NOBLEST OF THE SEDGES IS THE PAPYRUS, FROM WHICH in old time paper was made. It was once abundant, and was extensively cultivated, in Egypt, and is found now in the Sudan, also by the Sea of Galilee and Lake Huleh. The accounts of the process of making paper from it differ somewhat; but it was probably made by slicing the pith, and laying the slices side by side, and then placing another layer upon and across them, and pressing and drying the whole.

For the communication of thought by writing, it is necessary to assume some common plane of thought, some common standard in relation to the things to be told; or else they either cannot be told at all, or will be received in imperfect and distorted forms. And that common plane or standard of thought, which serves as a basis for the communication of definite ideas, is like the paper upon which characters are written. The noblest of the sedges, which represents a comprehensive knowledge of the standards of life and thought, furnished a suitable material for papermaking, in a primitive age when the standards were fairly natural.

The ark in which Moses was placed by his mother was "an ark of bulrushes," no doubt papyrus; because Moses represents the Divine law which was to be revealed through him; and this Divine law was to be brought down to the standard of life of the Egyptians and the Israelites; and the knowledge of that standard is represented by the ark of papyrus. It might also be represented by the book in which Moses wrote the law, which also was undoubtedly of papyrus (Deuteronomy 31:24; *Arcana Coelestia* §6723).

It was by the ark that Moses was kept alive, as was the Divine Truth by its being embodied in the morals and customs of the Jews. Without such embodiment it could not have been preserved; which was represented also by the breaking of the first tables of stone, and the necessity for the hewing out two others at the foot of the mount. These stones, however, represent the facts of the representative history, and the papyrus ark the plane of moral and natural life, in which the truth was embodied.

Reeds for Pens and Measurement

THE PAPER WAS MADE OF RUSHES, AND THE PENS WERE made of reeds. Reeds also, because they were straight, jointed, and light to carry, made convenient rods for measurement. Measuring reeds are several times mentioned in the Scriptures. Of these Swedenborg says:

> Divine Truth in the lowest degree, or in the ultimate of order, is such as is the Divine Truth in the sense of the letter of the Word, for children and the extremely simple. . . . This Divine Truth is what is signified by a reed or a cane. And because explorations are effected with all by means of this lowest Divine Truth . . . therefore measurings and weighings, in the representative churches, were performed by reeds or canes, by which that Divine Truth was signified. (*Apocalypse Explained* §627)

That definite ideas either of abstract truths or of history may be conveyed, there must be not only a knowledge of the common plane of thought and life, but a standard of what is right, or is assumed to be right, by which the quality of statements, persons, or events may be measured, and in relation to which they may be described. And this standard gives form to the record, like a pen upon the paper—the ink merely fixing that form, certifying to the truthfulness of the record to the measurement or the estimate. The reed with which John was commanded to measure the temple of God represented the standard of the acknowledgment of the Divine Human of the Lord and the life according to the commandments, by which the Christian heaven was to be measured.* Divine measurements are always made by a knowledge of the plainest Divine truth; and the record of them has form from their agreement or disagreement with that truth—the truth says they are so, or so. But human measurements and records of measurement, are according to human ideas of right and wrong, which may be the revealed standards or some very different standards. So far as they are the same, their record is in agreement with that in the Book of Life; but so far as they differ, they give false and deceptive measurements. "A reed shaken with the wind" the teaching of the letter of the Word is called, because the letter can be so turned hither and thither, and made to confirm various opinions.

If it be desired to mark the distinctions between the three families just described, it seems reasonable to regard the rushes as intelligence concerning what ought not to be done; the sedges as intelligence about what is done, or life as it is; and the reeds as intelligence concerning a just standard of life, and the measurement of other standards by it.

Sweet Cane

A SWEET OR AROMATIC CANE IS ALSO MENTIONED IN THE Word, and was one of the ingredients of the holy anointing oil, with which the priests and all the sacred things of

---

* In Swedenborgian studies, Divine Human or Divine Humanity refers to Jesus Christ after he put off the merely human things of all planes of his being and made them divine.

the tabernacle were anointed, and by virtue of which they were made holy, and representative of the Divine Human of the Lord. By this aromatic cane, we are taught, is signified "the perception and affection of interior truth" or "exterior truth in the internal man" (*Arcana Coelestia* §10256). Sweet odors signify what is delightful from spiritual affection; and this, applied to a reed, may signify the delight of agreement of the natural life and thought with the Divine truth, or the Divine standard of good and evil. This delight the Lord had in saying, "I do always those things that please Him" (John 8:29); "the Son can do nothing of Himself but what He seeth the Father do; for what things soever He doeth, these also doeth the Son likewise" (John 5:19).

FLAX AND COTTON

THESE TWO PLANTS FURNISH THE VEGETABLE FIBERS WITH which the greater part of mankind are clothed. The flax has a straight, branchless stalk, surmounted by pretty blue flowers; the stalk itself containing the fibers which are called linen when separated from the woody part, and spun into thread. The cotton plant is much branched, and bears many pods, which contain large, oily seeds enveloped in the mass of fibers which we call cotton wool. The fibers of linen are straight and shining; those of cotton are matted together; and, though equally white, are less silvery, and make warmer clothing.

It is not clear which of the two is meant by "linen" in the Bible, and perhaps both are meant, and it is not intended to distinguish between them. Neither does Swedenborg clearly distinguish; for he usually translates the Bible terms by "byssus" or "xylinum," and he says that "xylinum is byssus" (*Arcana Coelestia* §319); and that byssus, "which also is xylinum," "was a kind of whitest linen of which garments were made" (*Apocalypse Explained* §1143); apparently intending to be general, and not too specific, in his definition.

The Bible tells us of the armies in heaven following Him whose name is called the Word of God, "clothed in fine linen clean and white; for the fine linen is the just deeds of the saints." And Swedenborg tells us that when good spirits are instructed in the heavenly life, and taken up into heaven, "they are clothed in angelic garments, which are for the most part white as of linen" (*byssus, Heaven and Hell* §519). He has much to say about the correspondence of garments in heaven; and in general that they correspond to the intelligence of the angels, or truth in their external thought. The internal of angels and men is their love for what is to them good; but their external is made up of knowledge, and thought from knowledge in regard to what is good and true. The internal love is the living sensitive man; and the external knowledge and thought are like garments about the man in which he presents himself to others.

There are some angels who are simply loves for the Lord and the neighbor, not caring to know and think truth, but merely to live from good love. These best of the angels have not in them what corresponds to garments, and therefore need none. But others who love intelligent thought agreeing with good life appear in beautiful garments according to the quality of this thought (see *Apocalypse Explained* §240, 828). "All spirits and angels are clothed according to their intelligence. . . . The light of their intelligence is formed into garments, which, when they are formed thence, not only *appear* as garments, but also are garments" (*Apocalypse Explained* §395).

We are reminded that it is the Lord who covers Himself with light as with a garment (Psalm 104:2); and the internal of that light affects the minds of angels with intelligence, while the external clothes them with garments.

> In heaven, they who are in natural truth appear clothed in white, which appears like white linen; natural truth itself also is thus represented as if

132

woven of fine threads of linen; those threads appear like threads of silk, shining, beautifully translucent and soft, and the clothing made of them likewise, if the truth which is thus represented is from good; but, on the other hand, those threads like linen do not appear translucent, nor shining, nor soft, but hard and brittle, and yet white, if the truth so represented be not from good. (*Arcana Coelestia* §7601)

So much concerning the origin of linen-like garments in heaven has been presented, because it is the same power that forms them there which presses into the world to form similar substances here. There they are formed immediately, of spiritual elements; but here mediately, through the processes of natural growth. But the same love of intelligent thought about what is becoming and right in conduct which produces the garments of angels also, in the effort to produce similar garments here, becomes the life of the flax and the cotton, and actually forms the strong white fibers for clothing. The life of the blue-eyed, straight-stalked, shining flax, is the love of intelligent thought of what is straightforward, clean, and intelligent; and that of the warm and curly wool of the cotton, is the love for similar thought for what is kind and friendly as well as right.

In simpler days, the material of which paper was made was the pith of the papyrus plant. But now it is the worn out linen and cotton clothing of mankind. As the paper represents the common plane of life and thought which is assumed as the basis of communication, the papyrus represents a knowledge of such ways of life as are simple and natural. But when society became more complex and artificial, it became necessary to form a different plane by gathering a wide knowledge of the ways of life of many men and many nations, and generalizing it, and assuming that general knowledge as the basis of communication.

And so the linen and cotton rags are reduced to pulp, and made into white paper. The modern custom of making a common paper of wood pulp appears to have a correspondence with an assumed knowledge of the results of rational thought about all sorts of subjects, to which the trees correspond.

Together with these more artificial kinds of paper, there have come into use pens of various materials, quills and metals. And these appear to have a correspondence—the quills with the power of sustained thinking and comparison, such as is represented by the flight of birds—and the metals with knowledge of the laws of life. Such power and such knowledge determine the forms of statement and description.

The Tree of Life

The Bible begins with an account of a beautiful garden containing every tree that is pleasant to the sight and good for food; and in the midst of the garden was the Tree of Life. It closes with a description of a holy city, through the golden streets of which ran the river of water of life, and on either side of the river grew "the Tree of Life, bearing twelve manner of fruits, yielding her fruit every month, and the leaves of the tree were for the healing of the nations" (Revelation 22:2).

By the Garden of Eden is represented the innocent state of primeval man, taught by God, and wise from God in every work of heavenly love. By the Holy City is represented the state of man regenerated, returning with full rational development to the innocence of his childhood, to be wise again with the wisdom of the Lord, and to bring forth the fruits of the Divine Love for men (*Divine Providence* §313).

Every variety of Christian faith and love is represented by the twelve apostles and the twelve tribes of Israel; every variety of Christian usefulness, by the twelve kinds of fruit produced by the Tree of Life.

In the full sense every variety of intelligence and wisdom that looks to useful life lives from the Tree of Life which is in the midst of them all. Every tree that is good for food represents some wisdom of life that teaches good uses; every tree pleasant to the sight represents some intelligent knowledge that is a means of usefulness; herbs yielding seed that is good for food are the teaching of duties; and the grass and flowering herbage are the knowledge about good life by which the mind grows until it becomes mature and rational and can begin to do the good things which it has learned about. All these are of the wisdom of the Lord by which men live. They exist in every variety in the heavens, as to their spiritual essence, in the minds of angels and spirits; and as to their representative forms, in the paradises, the gardens, and fields which make heaven beautiful.

> In the inmost heaven . . . where love to the Lord reigns, their paradises and forests consist of olive yards and fig trees; but in the second heaven they consist of vineyards and various kinds of fruit trees; in like manner in the lowest heaven, but with this difference, that in this heaven the trees are not so noble. (*Apocalypse Explained* §638)

> In heaven there appear paradisiacal gardens with fruit trees according to the angels' wisdom from good of love from the Lord; but around those who are in intelligence and not in the good of love, there does not appear a garden, but grass; and around those who are in faith separate from charity, not even grass grows, but sand. (*Apocalypse Revealed* §90)

> They who have loved the sciences, and by them have cultivated their rational mind, and thus have procured for themselves intelligence, and at the

same time have acknowledged the Divine, have their pleasure in the sciences and rational enjoyment turned in the other life into spiritual enjoyment, which is of knowledge of what is good and true. They dwell in gardens, where there appear flower beds and grass plots beautifully laid out, and rows of trees round about, with porticos and walks; the trees and flowers being varied from day to day. The sight of all in general brings joys to their minds, and the varied particulars continually renew them. And because these correspond to Divine things, and they are acquainted with correspondences, they are continually filled with new knowledges, and thereby their spiritual-rational is perfected. These are their enjoyments, because gardens, flower beds, grass plots, and trees correspond to sciences, knowledges, and intelligence therefrom. (*Heaven and Hell* §489)

The influence of heaven is continually descending to the earth, and operating both upon the minds of men and upon the substances of nature, in the effort to produce upon the earth forms of the Divine Life like those in heaven. In heaven they exist in a fullness of interior perfection and variety that is not possible in the grosser atmospheres and earths of the natural world. Here the innumerable varieties of heaven can only be expressed in generals. Yet the Holy City is a church upon the earth, corresponding to the heavens; and the Tree of Life which grows in that city is the Divine Wisdom of Life, as received by the men of the Church. Its fruits are the good works which they who know and love the Lord will do from Him for one another—the works of the Lord's Providence done by Him through men; and its leaves are the rational perceptions of what conduces to good life by which they who live "in evils and in falsities will be led to think soundly and to live becomingly" (*Apocalypse Revealed* §936). And whatever of the Tree of Life is implanted in the natural life in this world, has in it the possibility of endless devel - opment in heaven—of wisdom and usefulness and a sense of life from the Lord, with all the beautiful external cre- ations which correspond to these things.

WATER

WATER IS THE MEANS OF MOTION TO ALL THE MATERIALS of the earth, and the medium of communication between the air and the earth. It partakes of the nature of both; on the one hand being readily resolvable into oxygen and hydrogen, and also mingling with the air in its own aerial form of vapor, and on the other, having the weight and substantial character of a mineral, and in the form of ice, some of the hardness of the rocks.

It is the privilege of water to give motion to the materials which plants desire for food. The offerings of the earth cannot be absorbed by the roots except in solution; the water, therefore, introduces them through the spongy doors, and conducts them up the staircase of wood to the leaves. In the leaves it receives also the nutritive portions of the atmosphere admitted through their little windows, and holds all subject to the action of the sunshine, and of the vital forces of the plant. When thoroughly prepared, it bears the digested food to the fruit and the wood for their increase.

The same excellent office it performs in the economy of the animal kingdom: it gives mobility, through arteries and veins and all proper tissues, to the various materials which nourish the body and compose its secretions and excretions. Abstract it from any part, and that part becomes dead as a chip; diminish it in any considerable degree throughout the body, and the sluggish fluids refuse to respond to the vital impulses of the spirit; so that the spirit must needs separate itself from them and cast them off.

The bountifulness of the supply of water and the perfection of the means provided for its distribution show its importance in the eyes of Him who provides it. Everywhere it drops from the clouds—originally, no doubt, the whole descended from the watery atmosphere—and, after supplying the immediate wants of every living thing, and filling the earth and every reservoir and crevice that can hold it, it runs merrily off in brooks and rivers, giving motion now to mills and logs and boats, and finally mingles with the sea. Nor does it there rest in idleness, but enters the great system of ocean currents, which cool the tropics, extend the habitable zones to the north and the south, and undoubtedly contribute much, in ways that are still obscure, to the healthfulness of the earth for human habitation. In the ocean, too, it bears up the ships, and serves as a means of communication among all the countries of the earth.

Invited from the ocean by the air and sunshine, it enters upon a new sphere of usefulness. In the very act of expand - ing into vapor, it absorbs the excessive heat of the air, which it is ready at any moment to restore, if desired, assuming again for itself the form of dew or frost, rain, snow, or hail. Besides equalizing the temperature of the air, it softens its otherwise too drying contact with plants and animals, and combining with its nutritive materials, accommodates them to the uses of life. At the same time it deepens the blue of the sky, renders the air clearer, and holds the impurities in readiness to be carried off by the rain.

It is a little difficult to put one's finger upon the spiritual correlative of this admirable substance, and hold it for examination, on account of its transparency and mobility. But if we were consuming with fever and thirst, we should be likely to recognize the natural element which we need. Suppose, then, that we are burning with spiritual fever, our affections are excited by the apprehension of a great injury or misfortune, we are restless, eager, and feverish with anxiety. A friend comes in, cool and quiet, brings out some hopeful points in the situation, shows what is unreasonable in our feelings, and presents clearly the right and practicable thing to do. If we are sane, the restless burning will be quieted, and we shall set about what it is possible for us to do, in a healthy manner. Possibly our friend's practical advice is spiritual water; at any rate, a liberal application of such common sense to unwise zeal is familiarly called "pouring cold water" over it. In this case the spiritual element employed is truth which discriminates between good and evil, between the practicable and the impracticable, and sets the thoughts running in useful channels. The common expression, "thirst for knowledge," as applied to spiritual thirst, so far appears to be justified, with the qualification that this particular kind of knowledge is understood.

Let us see whether this will answer to the other uses and conditions of water, or what modification of our definition, if any, is required. And first, if it be true spiritual water, it is not only useful in feverish states, but is a daily necessity to the life of the mind. The food of the mind is knowledge of good and pleasant things, and of all things that increase its affection and desire. When the mind is nourished by such food, and good desires are strong in it, it inquires immediately what it is right and practicable for it to do. The knowledge it already has is good and pleasant, but it cannot live from it, nor even take it into active consideration, and so assimilate it, till a knowledge of what is practicable and right sets it flowing. The same spiritual element seems here to meet the requirement.

But food must be combined with water, that it may be tasted and received at all, not only that it may circulate through the body. Perfectly dry food on a dry tongue has no taste and cannot be swallowed. And so the knowledge of good things, which is food to the mind, cannot be received till it is brought into some sort of relation to us; if perfectly dry and uninteresting to us, we reject it. And it is brought into relation to us by a knowledge of what is universally right and useful, which is like water drunk with it; or, better still, by a knowledge of what is right and useful to us, which mingles with the food, and moistens it as with our own saliva. This brings out the real quality of the seeming good in its relation to us, and we know whether or not it is agreeable to our life.

Another important use of water, very different apparently, and yet performed by its power of giving mobility, is in washing. The soiling matter, which in its dry state clings to the garments or the skin, is separated by water, which penetrates between the filth and the organized substance, gives wheels to the loosened particles, and trundles them off. Spiritual defilement, we are taught, is from thinking and doing evil—from "evil thoughts, murders, adulteries, fornications, thefts, false witness, blasphemies." And when the spirit is defiled by thinking these, or by affection for them, the means of cleansing is manifestly the truth which shows these things to be hurtful and wrong. Such truth, if fairly applied, separates the particles from the mind, and carries them off.

It is because this practical repentance is spiritual washing that baptism, which represents it, is the appointed sign of introduction into the Church.

Rightly received, it is an expression of desire and resolve to purify the life according to the truth into which one is baptized; and therefore it admits the recipient to the society of men and angels who are in the same effort, and entitles him to their assistance.

The same is signified by the entrance to the Land of Canaan through the River Jordan, and also by John's baptizing in the Jordan. And, for a similar reason, washings of the body and the clothes were a prominent part of the Jewish ceremonial.

But this that we are now speaking of is knowledge of hurtfulness and wrong, and we were before considering the knowledge of what is useful and right, which appears to be a different thing. The difference, however, is only in appearance; for a knowledge of what is right gives the means of recognizing what is not right, and of judging it justly according to its opposition to the right. The truth which teaches what is useful to be done shows also what is to be shunned. Thus the difference is not in the truth, but in the application of it.

In the Apocalypse John says, "And He showed me a pure river of water of life, clear as crystal, proceeding out of the throne of God and of the Lamb." By this pure river, Swedenborg tells us, is meant "the Apocalypse now opened and explained as to its spiritual sense, where Divine truths are revealed in abundance from the Lord, for those who will be in His New Church, which is the New Jerusalem."

In the Apocalypse are now laid open the evils and falsities of the Church, which must be shunned and held in aversion, and the goods and truths of the Church which must be done, especially concerning the Lord, and concerning eternal life from Him, which are meant in particular by the pure river of water of life, clear as crystal, proceeding out of the throne of God and of the Lamb. (*Apocalypse Revealed* §932)

Another difficulty which may appear serious is that we seem to be confounding right and wrong with practicability or expediency; whereas these seem to be quite distinct, since a given course of conduct may be entirely practicable, but wholly wrong. But it must be remembered that water is not in itself fixed and rigid like iron and stone, but yields and adapts itself to things which are fixed. Neither is it exclusive in its associations; it laves, with equal readiness, golden quartz and the slime of the docks, and ministers alike to the olive tree and the humblest moss. Spiritual water, likewise, is neither law nor fact, but the truth of life under all the circumstances of any case. We call that "practicable" which considers the external circumstances, and that "right" which considers the Divine laws. Spiritual water considers either, or both, when both enter into the case. It teaches a man how to repent of his sins, and to do his duties to God and his fellow men; it teaches him also how to build his house under the conditions of the laws of health, and how to conduct his business under the laws of economy and honesty. It teaches the little bird how to protect her featherless young from the storm; it leads the wild goat to conceal her kids among the mountain crags, and the lioness to make her den in the thickets; it guides the salmon, in breeding time, up the rivers, and shows the butterflies where their offspring will find suitable food; it causes the flowers to expand their delicate petals to the sunlight, teaching some to fold them up again at the approach of cold or wet. It is just as essential to Nature in carrying out her ideas as it is to man. Solid fact and fixed law we shall find in the rocks and metals; it is not these. It is truth which, adapting itself to every variety of circumstances, shows what can be done in those circumstances, under the impulse of a given desire. It does not alter the nature of the truth, that animals obey it "instinctively," and plants perhaps "mechanically," and man conscientiously and thoughtfully; it is the same natural truth of life to all, showing what is wise or unwise, right or wrong, in their respective situations.

Almost colorless itself, it appears everywhere in the colors of the subjects to which it is applied. In general forms of knowledge of life, it takes the color of our mental skies, reflecting the clear blue of Infinite Intelligence, or the dullness of human obscurity; in relation to particular men or masses of men, it takes their colors, and is formed by their circumstances; regarded as the truth of Nature, we see it in all the bright colors of natural life. In Nature, it is the wisdom of Nature; in affairs of the world it is practical wisdom; in moral affairs it is the truth of right and wrong; in history it is the wisdom of experience; in Scripture it is the wisdom of revelation. No useful life is possible without it. It enters into every development of intelligence, every theory, every plan of life. It is the living part of our knowledge of history and of natural history, of the works of God and the works of men. The waters are as important and abundant in our mental world as in the physical; and we shall find them subject to corresponding influences, appearing in corresponding forms, and doing corresponding uses in every particular.

Salt

NOT ONLY DOES WATER TAKE ITS COLOR AND SHAPE FROM the objects about it, as has been shown, but some of them it dissolves in greater or less degree, and with them modifies its own quality. It dissolves little from the rocks; but salts of various kinds, sugar, and many other vegetable substances it takes up readily. And so, likewise, from a fixed, unchangeable truth, as that light and heat are from the sun, the truth of life takes almost nothing. It plays about it like water at the foot of a rock, filling itself with its colors, and adapting itself to its form; it says, "Because this is so, you must make windows in your houses, and open them towards the sun"; but it does not presume to say that the fact itself is right or wrong, practicable or impracticable. But other truths which contain suggestions as to ways of doing good—suggestions of sweetness, tartness, pungency, or other quality, are readily incorporated in the thought of life. The most important of these is the principle that goodness and truth need each other and belong together, which is the correlative of common salt. Fixed as this is, and crystalline, the truth of life recognizes it as akin to itself, incorporates it readily into itself, and suggests everywhere to inquirers how to do good, that it must be done according to the truth. The rain that soaks through the earth, receives the particles of the earth which are most ready to unite with it, the chief element in which is common salt, and carries them to the sea, in token of the readiness of the earth to unite with the water, and of its own desire to unite with the earth in fruitfulness. With the salt we season our food, to express its willingness to unite with the fluids of the body, and this willingness is to our perception savoriness. But, when received, the salt in the body excites thirst, which is like the desire of the earth for water, and represents a deficiency of truth of life. When this is excessive, life ceases; whence came the custom in ancient times of sowing with salt the cities which were doomed to desolation—representing their lack of truth of life.

The Sea

THE SEAS OF OUR MINDS ARE THE MEMORY OF ALL THE truth of life we have seen. They are salt because there is with the truth the memory of its varied applications.

The seas, and other large bodies of water, are homes for the fishes; and spiritual fishes are affections for thinking in the truth of Nature and of natural life, and accumulating knowledge of it. By such accumulation they furnish food to affections for spiritual life and thought.

These large bodies of water afford, also, the means of transportation and intercommunication to all the countries bordering upon the same water. The ships, by which such communication is effected, are substantial houses built to sail upon the water. Spiritually, they are doctrines which teach the proper relation and subordination of natural truth and life to spiritual. They rest upon natural truth, but interpret it to the support of spiritual life and its enjoyments. They resist the misapplication of natural truth, as ships resist storms, and insist upon its proper subordination. From such a ship the Lord taught of the heavenly life to people who before knew no other than the common truth of natural life. From it He quieted the waves of turbulent natural thought, and reduced them to orderly service. The commerce of the earth carried on in ships corresponds to the interchange of the good things of spiritual life among those who have a common knowledge of good and evil.

The currents of the ocean have been mentioned, which bring the coolness of the poles to the tropics, and return the warmth of the tropics far towards the poles. And from memory and history, in like manner, come the currents of cooler truth to allay the heat of popular excitement, or of warmer truth to restore confidence in states of discouragement. That there is such an interchange among the nations of the earth is probable.

The Clouds of Heaven

WHAT ONE LOVES SUPREMELY, OR WORSHIPS AS THE HIGHest good, is to him his god. Under its influence he forms his ideas of the spiritual nature of man, and of the eternal state of the spirit, selecting for that purpose from his general knowledge of human life, as the sun raises water from the seas and the earth into the air. It is written in Genesis that God made an "expanse, and divided the waters which were under the expanse from the waters which were above the expanse, and it was so. And God called the expanse heaven." The waters under the expanse are the knowledge of life in this world; the waters above the expanse are the knowledge of the life of the spirit and of eternity. The truth of life in the Scriptures, regarded as relating to actions in this world, is water under the expanse; but, looked upon as a revelation from God concerning the life of the spirit here and hereafter, it rests above the firmament towards the heaven of our mind, like clouds in the sky. To the Scriptures, thus regarded, we go for the things which belong to heaven, and which help us into a heavenly state. We find there the light in which the God of heaven sees, and by which He enlightens the minds of men; and thence also we obtain positive ideas of a future life and of the utterly different states of the good and the evil in it.

But the Scriptures, regarded spiritually, are not merely a revelation of another world; they relate also to the state of the spirit in this world. The truth of right and useful life is as applicable to the mind as to the body; for what it is wrong to do, it is wrong to think of doing, or to desire to do. The same truth cleanses both works and thoughts. To love it, think it, and apply it to the thoughts makes our spiritual atmosphere cleaner and brighter, and removes from it the obscurities between us and the Lord. When we read the Scriptures for the sake of learning to live better, and to be better throughout, the truth which shows us what it is right to do and think falls gently into the mind, cleansing its thought and encouraging every principle of life, like fertilizing showers upon the earth. And when our desire is satisfied, as the rain ceases, and we go on thinking the truth, the cloud dissolves, and becomes a part of the air we breathe, and through the pure, blue heaven comes the glad sunshine of the Lord's immediate presence.

It is in this way that our Lord is coming in the clouds of heaven; for all the precepts and instructions in the Word, when opened interiorly by means of correspondences, are pure, spiritual truth concerning good life in relation to the Lord, and to the spiritual states of men; we have only to love it for the sake of thoroughly good life, and the letter disappears, while the spirit is to us as the breath of heaven.

At the time of His first coming, the disciples were not able to think spiritually; they were simple, natural men, who could receive instruction in regard to their natural duties, but must have their spiritual truth clothed in parables and proverbs, or they could not receive it. The Lord showed Himself to three of the disciples in the mount, His face shining as the sun, and His raiment white as the light; but they could not spiritually awake to see Him; they were heavy with sleep; nor did they recover their powers of thought until after a cloud overshadowed them.

Centuries before, when the previous revelation of the Lord was made to their ancestors, so gross and material were their ideas of Him and His kingdom that the mountain between Him and them smoked like a furnace, with darkness, clouds, and thick darkness.

And to go back one step more, to the days when the men of the earliest Church turned wholly away from the Lord, and believed themselves to be gods, the dire falseness of their ideas of their spiritual nature and future life, from which came the most abominable works and principles, was represented by the heavens from whose windows come the waters of the flood which swept them all away.

Streams

IT IS CHARACTERISTIC OF WATER, THAT WHEN IT FALLS from the clouds it runs down the hills to the plains, and then further, seeking the lowest level. And so the truth of what is right and useful, when received in elevated states of mind, immediately sets itself to run through all the states of the life, everywhere purifying, nourishing, and urging to good works; nor will it rest till, the whole active productive part of the mind traversed, it finds repose in the sea of the memory. If the state in which the truth is received be greatly elevated above the common plane of the life, the truth descends with vehemence, and possibly great power for good. But from minds that are self-exalted, especially if they be hard and stony—not inclined to do quiet uses themselves—it descends with angry vehemence, and great power for evil; these throw off the truth from themselves, and direct it in pitiless torrents to those whom they look down upon. Such streams received by many minds at once form great rivers of public opinion, which serve as a medium of communication among all who share them; which, wisely directed, set powerful social machinery in motion for good; or, angrily swelling, sweep away much that is good, with some evil, in a common ruin.

On the other hand, a mind full of earnest affection for good holds the truth received from heaven as a good soil does the rain, giving it forth slowly and steadily in useful springs and streams of truth.

Ice

A CERTAIN DEGREE OF LOVE FOR THE LORD, OR FOR THE neighbor, is necessary to keep the streams of thought concerning good life running. In a state of indifference and coldness we cease to apply it to life, and our collected stores of truth exist only as hard fixed knowledge of what we have been thinking, or have perceived to be true. Our streams are frozen to ice, till the returning love of use sets them flowing again. In our cool state we do not make much use of the truth; still, we take an intellectual pleasure in skimming over it, as upon skates or sleighs, and use it as a common ground of communication with others—

all the more readily for our want of tenderness towards it. We also use it when any immoderate zeal or passion, as of summer heat or fever, is excited, which, by the application of cool passionless truth, is tempered down to healthful moderation.

Dew

WHEN THE SUN GOES DOWN IN A CLEAR, BRIGHT SKY— full of moisture, as a very clear sky always is—the leaves and the grass, and the surface of the ground, as they cool, condense the moisture in little drops all over themselves, from which they drink as much as they will for their refreshment, and keep themselves warm with the rest. And so at the end of a state of labor in which the mind has been intently thinking and loving spiritual truth, with repose come pleasant views of the work of life, of friends, and of the community, suggesting everywhere useful applications of the truth we have been thinking and loving. Every growing plant in the mind is revived by such perceptions, and though not warmed by the immediate presence of the sun, is kept from losing too much of its heat by the delight of knowing the truth.

The dew is "sweeter and pleasanter than showers," Swedenborg says, "whence the grass and the crops of the fields are gladdened." "The truth of peace," he calls it, spiritually; and says that "it is the Divine truth from the Lord in heaven, and affects universally all who are there, and makes heaven to be heaven" (*Arcana Coelestia* §8455).

Hoarfrost is the dew made white and solid by cold. It is the "truth of peace" regarded as a good thing in itself, and not applied at once to good uses (*Arcana Coelestia* §8459).

Snow

SNOW IS FROZEN CLOUD, WHICH FALLS PURE AND WHITE upon the earth, gently covering it from cold, and preserving its life till the sun renews its energies. When the zeal for use is past, and the mind needs rest, relapsing into a quiet natural state, with no thought of work, there may still be delight in learning truth, which is then loved for its own beauty, and as a good thing in itself; it is, like the snow, white, beautiful, comparatively solid, and may be accumulated. It keeps the mind from cooling down into evil and death, by interesting it in the truth as an object of desire, and thus preserving its vitality as a garment does the warmth of the body.

In this form, truth affords easy means of communication and transportation; for, in this comparatively cool state, we meet others easily on the common ground of intellectual delight in truth alone; and the stores of experience and useful love, which we might not be able to communicate when the affections are warmer, may be readily produced and imparted.

Truths of moral philosophy, proverbs, pithy sayings as to what men do or ought to do, may be ice in various forms. Similar truth as to wisdom of life from the Bible may be snow from heaven; as when one says abstractly, the Bible regards this or that as right or wrong. Such truth as to the Bible standards may be accumulated indefinitely.

When recalled in warmer states, these stores of truth may be most useful to spiritual fruitfulness; for, "As the rain cometh down, and the snow, from heaven, and returneth not thither, but watereth the earth, and maketh it bring forth and bud, that it may give seed to the sower and bread to the eater, so shall my word be that goeth forth out of my mouth" (Isaiah 55:10, 11).

Hail

HAIL IS RAIN CARRIED UP SO HIGH THAT IT IS FROZEN, and then pelted down to the destruction of tender plants. Yet, when melted, it turns to rainwater. It is like truths of the Word carried up by intense conceit into its own state of great self-exaltation, made hard by the total absence of charity, and cast at men as truths of a pitiless Divine Justice. When interpreted and softened by kindness, these same truths may be melted into gentle, beneficent truth of life.

Steam

A MOST INTERESTING DEVELOPMENT OF THE USE OF WATER has occurred in our day, in the universal application of steam to machinery. The locomotive, running over smoothly laid iron rails, brings even more than the utmost fleetness of the horse to the general service of mankind. Applied to ships upon the sea, the moving power of steam equally surpasses that of the wind; and in connection with stationary machinery, it increases the working power of man a hundredfold.

The boiling of the waters is mentioned in Isaiah as an illustration of the effect of the Lord's coming: "Oh, that Thou wouldst rend the heavens, that Thou wouldst come down, that the mountains might flow down at Thy presence, as when the melting fire burneth, the fire causeth the waters to boil!" (Isaiah 64:1, 2). And as the comparisons in the Scriptures are not mere comparisons, but correspondences as well, we should expect, in the fulfillment of the words, that the Divine love of the Lord, when His presence is manifested, would expand, with Infinite interior meaning, all the natural truth of His creation and His revelation. And so, indeed, it is. But we should hardly have looked for so literal a fulfillment, also, as the effect of His coming in the clouds of heaven.

The natural work of the steam is simply a correspondence of the spiritual work of that which steam represents. The opening of the spiritual meanings in natural truth affects the mind with a delight and a power for good, which is not more than adequately represented by the expansive force of steam. Beautiful thoughts are multiplied by it, and the ability to render helpful service to the souls of men is greatly increased.

Especially does the opening of spiritual truth give the means of understanding those in quite dissimilar states; it shows the unity of mankind, in the widest variety; and because of that unity it interests us in states the most remote from our own, and prepares the way for mutually advantageous intercourse.

The days are not yet long past in which it was impossible for conscientious people who held different religious views to have any communication with one another, or even to live peaceably in the same country.

An improvement has already taken place, to the extent of establishing a basis of mutual toleration and natural justice among many nations and religions, which may be likened to the building of good roads; but there is as yet scarcely any of the opening of interior things, which we may fairly expect to make the communications of the future so interesting and profitable.

That the approach of the Lord should produce first a development of natural philanthropy and intelligence, before the corresponding increase of spiritual wisdom and love, is according to the Lord's prediction: "Behold the fig tree and all the trees."

We may confidently accept the natural work that has been accomplished, both as a manifestation of the mighty spiritual power which is present, and as a sign that the spiritual work will shortly be brought to pass.

THE ROCKS AND METALS

Rocks

THE ROCKS HAVE MANY POINTS OF RESEMBLANCE TO WATER; so many that water is ranked among them as a mineral. They agree in their differences from sensitive animals and growing plants. But rocks are utterly unlike water in their hardness, inflexibility, and solidity.

We found the spiritual correlative of water in the general truth which shows what is good and practicable in any given case—truth which is universal, applicable to all circumstances, and taking its quality in great degree from circumstances. The rocks of the mind must be principles that are fixed, unyielding, and nearly unchangeable.

Such principles there are of many kinds. There is an immense quantity of truth concerning things that have been done; which truth is now fixed, and not subject to change. This may be called historical truth. When it is really fixed, it is solid, inflexible, and to be depended upon, like the stones. Another kind of truth, still more extensive than that of history, is the fixed truth of natural history. It is such truth as that the sun gives heat; that grains and fruits are nutritious; that lambs are innocent; that birds have nests; that the morning always follows the night, and summer the winter. There is an immense variety of truth like this that is in the very nature of things, and it is the foundation of all theories, plans, and works.

All this fixed truth of natural history and of history has the general characteristics of rock. It is hard, solid, and unyielding; we trust to it, and build upon it and with it, in a manner exactly corresponding to our use of stones.

Stones are inflexible, but they can be broken or cut so that larger or smaller fragments may be taken for use. The facts of history, likewise, are not easily bent out of their natural forms, but they may readily be subdivided, and such portions of them taken as are wanted. The fixed truths of nature also are inflexible, but may be opened by well-directed effort, and examined in their details. It is a comprehensive truth of this kind that the earth attracts towards itself all material bodies. We readily separate from this general truth the particulars that the earth attracts this falling stone or these fluttering leaves; for this mental stone has been so long exposed to the wear of human thought that its surface is easily pulverized. It is more difficult to see that the earth extends her attractive power to the sun, the planets, and the stars.

Another nobler rock is the truth that the Lord's Providence is over all the events of life. This rock lies deep, but not too deep for the knowledge of those whose lives are deeply founded; yet even they separate from the rock the particulars, and see that the Divine Providence is in this or that event, only by considerable effort.

Roads

OF BROKEN STONES WE MAKE OUR ROADS, WHICH BY USE become smooth and hard, suited for walking, riding, or the transportation of heavy loads. Spiritual distance is difference of state. And spiritual roads are the ways by which we pass from our own familiar states of thought and feeling to the states of others like or unlike our own. If there be an abundance of fact, or of certain truth, more or less common, which reaches our neighbor's state as well as our own, and which we both are familiar with, or take for granted because of its general use, it is easy to pass from one state to the other, and to interchange the good things of both. If the truths we depend upon are new to us, and it is necessary to observe and recognize them separately, the way is tedious, and progress in coming together is slow, as by a freshly dressed road. Or if there be individual truths that we have to stop to explain away, and especially if they arrest the whole attention and refuse to be explained away, our road is obstructed, perhaps altogether closed, by misplaced stones.

Soil

THE ROCKS, FINELY PULVERIZED, MAKE THE GREATER PART of the soil, and in this condition they give support to plants and trees. The particles of the soil correspond to the little particulars of natural truth which we are obliged to depend upon and to use in the plans for work and for pleasure of every day's life. No plan can be formed without building into itself some particulars of truth of nature, which, when the present need has passed, may serve for others; as there is no plant but has its mineral ash which, when the plant decays, is food for other plants.

Millstones

OF THE ROCKS WE MAKE MILLSTONES, BY WHICH THE GRAINS are broken and ground into flour for bread. In this work millstones perform a similar use to that of the teeth, which are little millstones for laying open the interior parts of food. Upon the lower millstone the grain rests as it passes from the hopper, and the upper stone revolving lays open and separates all its particles. Grains are the works of everyday duty, more or less noble according to the principles of life of those who do them, and more or less filled with thought and affection for the neighbor. The works not understood do not nourish the souls of men; but examined and known as to the affection and thought within them, they do give comfort and strength to human hearts. To examine them thoroughly, we need a lower millstone of general truth about the states and circumstances under which the works were done; and an upper, movable millstone about what it would be natural for us to do under such conditions. And this we need to apply to the works under consideration, bringing out the thought and feeling that entered into them.

Millers know that after long use their millstones become smooth and blunted, so that the grain passes through them imperfectly ground. And so by friction in the world, our fundamental principles of human nature and human life become worn and glossed over, so that we pass many things in a conventional way, without examining them sufficiently to get hold of their true quality. And then we need to attend to our principles, to break up their worldly easiness, and to bring out their crystalline surfaces of genuine truth, which will examine thoroughly and judge rightly.

Pottery

Of stone were formerly made jugs and pitchers for water; and nowadays these, and a thousand other vessels for containing food and drink, are made of clay hardened to stone by fire. These vessels are the facts of our daily wants, which formerly were few and simple, and fashioned from the truth of nature; but now are many and artificial formed from the truth of usage and fashion merely, hardened by our love for it into fixed customs. These, however, are easily broken when genuine truth of nature is applied to them; but even then, their fragments are almost indestructible—facts of what life has been.

Deposited and Crystalline Rocks

The clay of which pottery is made is itself originally derived from the primitive rocks. By the action of ice and water, particles and larger fragments are continually separated from the rocks, and by their own friction they disengage other fragments. These, borne by the running water into seas or inland lakes, are deposited, the larger bits early in beds of gravel or sand, the smaller, because they unite more intimately with the water, more remotely in beds of clay; and these beds, if undisturbed, are hardened by Nature's slow, gigantic kiln—the sand into sandstone, the clay into slate.

In the domain of mind we trace the corresponding process. The primitive rocks are the fixed truths of nature; running water is the truth which shows what is good, right, and useful, under any given circumstances. This truth, as men receive it, is directed and guided by the fixed truth of nature—as, for example, that it is not practicable to use stones for bread, or fruits for building; and it is continually incorporating with itself such bits as show what is possible or impossible as that when we are hungry we must eat what is soft and nutritious; and by the comparison of these again with the original mass of truth, it detaches more particulars—as that grains are edible, and are made more so by cooking; fruits, also, in various degrees. The great streams which bear onward these bits of natural truth are the thoughts and lives of communities; the lakes and seas to which they are borne, are the various forms of memory and history; the water of the seas is the truth which men have lived; and the deposited beds of stone are the portions of fundamental truth which they have received and worked into their lives, and which now constitute the facts of their lives.

In such deposited rock are imbedded in great numbers the remains of plants and animals, both those that have been washed down from the land, and those that lived in the water; and so history preserves to us the biographies of individual men, imbedded like fossils in the mass of general knowledge of what was done and thought in their time. Especially do we have preserved mementos of the historians and the accumulators of knowledge; for these are like inhabitants of the sea, delighting in the knowledge to which the sea corresponds, and identifying themselves with it.

There are some beds of rock, as various kinds of limestone, which are made altogether of the remains of animals; the beds of coal, on the other hand, are composed of vegetable remains. To study them all would be to explore the whole spiritual history of mankind—a delightful subject, indeed, to pursue, and one that will yield precious returns of spiritual knowledge to future students of correspondences.

From what has already been said, however, we are prepared to interpret the distinction between the stratified rocks, which were deposited underwater, and which cover nearly the whole of the rock surface of the earth, and the underlying rocks, mostly crystalline, and bearing the marks of intense heat, which usually appear upon the surface only among high hills and mountains. The latter are the truths of nature and of human nature, as God made them and as they really are. The former are these truths as men have understood them and lived them.

These two kinds of rock, where they come in contact, cannot readily be distinguished from each other, many crystalline rocks having been originally deposited, and then modified by heat or by hot water. The correlative truth is that even the truths of nature took form by degrees, as nature itself came into form, and the order of its operations became established. For instance, the truth that birds produce their young from eggs did not always exist; for birds did not always exist. But when birds were created they began to lay eggs, and from the little isolated facts of one and another having laid eggs, soon grew up the crystalline truth that they always produce their young from eggs.

In mountains the fundamental rocks rise far above the common level, sometimes bearing upon their slopes the stratified rocks, and sometimes rising above them. They lift their heads even among the clouds, which cling about them with special fondness, continually watering them with pure rain and snow from heaven, and sending down their rocky sides life and power and fruitfulness to the country all around.

Upon such fundamental spiritual rocks as that the world, created by God, is from humanity and for humanity; that the existence of the world is its continual creation, and that the Lord's Providence rules every particle in it; upon such rocks as these we rise, often with many less perfect traditional ideas, far above the ordinary level of life, to a height where the spiritual atmosphere is clear and pure, where we think and see truly, and where we drink of the water of life directly from the Lord through the clouds of His Word. It is well for the spiritual and moral welfare of all, that such truths as these are acknowledged by some.

Precious Stones

THE FACTS WHICH WE HAVE BEEN CONSIDERING ABOUT the rocks are distinct clearly defined truths about the very nature of the things. They are crystals, most of them opaque, yet reflecting obscurely the light of spiritual truth. But there are also precious stones which are distinguished from common stones by their hardness and by their beautiful colors, or the brilliancy of the light which they transmit. They are truths in natural forms, from which or through which the light of spiritual wisdom shines clearly.

When Peter confessed to the Lord, "Thou art the Christ, the Son of the Living God," the Lord replied, "Upon this rock I will build my Church." This confession is, indeed, the foundation of the Christian Church; but it is no dull, opaque rock. It is open to the light of the Sun of heaven, and to those who love that light it is full of heavenly beauty. We need not wonder that the broad foundation of the Church is a precious stone. All the foundations of the Holy City are precious stones; her streets are pure gold, and her gates are pearls.

The Lord's Word is full of jewels, finer, purer, more enduring, more full of light, than any other stones. All our spiritual life rests upon such certain truths as these:

I and my Father are One. (John 10:30)

He whom God hath sent speaketh the words of God. (John 3:34)

I am the Living Bread that came down from heaven. (John 6:51)

That which is born of the flesh is flesh, and that which is born of the spirit is spirit. (John 3:6)

Whosoever shall do the will of God, the same is my brother and sister and mother. (Mark 3:35)

God so loved the world that He gave His only begotten Son, that whosoever believeth in Him should not perish, but have everlasting life. (John 3:16)

Every good tree bringeth forth good fruit; but a corrupt tree bringeth forth evil fruit. (Matthew 7:17)

Among such jewels, those that reveal the love of the Lord for man, and the reciprocal love of men for the Lord, if presented to our spiritual sight as gems, would shine with warm light as the ruby, the carbuncle, and the sardius. Those that show the clear light of the Divine Wisdom would shine like clear crystal, or like the diamond. Those that treat of the love of wisdom in angels and men, according to the quality and the purpose of the wisdom loved, might appear in a variety of colors, like those of the sapphire, the sardonyx, the beryl, or the jacinth; for these colors represent such heavenly affections.

Metals

AMONG THE ROCKS WE FIND METALS; THE MOST NOBLE OF them, as gold and silver, especially among crystalline rocks. Metals differ from stone in that they can be bent, beaten out, and molded; they also melt easily, and can be cast into every desired shape. They are opaque, but when pure they reflect light brilliantly, and if polished may be used as mirrors. Of them are made coins, ornaments, plate, and tools of every kind—agricultural, domestic, mechanical, and warlike.

As stones are definite and certain truth which cannot readily yield or change, metals are truth as firm and indestructible, but taking definite form from circumstances. For instance, it is a truth, as unchangeable as rock, that fire is hot and burning. That rock naturally gives rise to the truth that if you put any combustible thing into the fire it will be burned; which truth may be molded into various forms, as that you must not bring precious things near the fire, or they will be burned; that the fire must be carefully confined, or it will endanger the house; and these necessary forms of a stern natural law are exactly embodied in fenders and stoves and fire utensils of iron.

But this law is of a comparatively low kind. It is a nobler law that the good of a community, and the real good of individuals, can be obtained only by the yielding of individual selfish preferences. It is a law nobler still, that genuine happiness is found in serving others, never in serving oneself. And it is a more precious law than all these that the Lord expressed in the words, "If a man love Me, he will keep my words; and My Father will love him, and We will come unto him, and make our abode with him" (John 14:23).

Laws of life of all these kinds, natural, moral, spiritual, and heavenly, correspond to the metals. They in some degree resemble water, in that their form may be changed to fit the subject treated of. But when they are applied to any given subject, they are inflexible and durable as the stones themselves. The law that you must not put your unprotected hand into the fire, or it will be burned, is just as unchangeable as the crystalline truth that fire is hot and burning; but the substance of the law could be remolded and applied to any other combustible thing, just as well as to your hand.

In molten form the metals, like water, apply themselves to the conditions at hand, saying that under those conditions one may do thus. But as they cool, they harden into fixed usages.

The kinds of truth which correspond respectively to the most important metals, and the peculiar characteristics of each, are fully illustrated by Swedenborg's description of the angels from the ages called golden, silver, copper, and iron;* so called because such was the character of their principles of life. In visiting them, he inquired particularly concerning their marriages; and as are the principles of marriage, so are all the principles of life.

---

* The Most Ancient Church, Ancient Church (silver and bronze), and Jewish or Israelitish Church, respectively.

Gold

AN EXPERIENCE AMONG THE ANGELS OF THE EARLIEST
people upon our earth—a people whose innocent communion with God is remembered in the traditions of all
races:

> I looked by turns, on the husband and wife, and
> observed as it were the unity of their souls in their
> faces; and I said, "You are one." And the man
> answered, "We are one; her life is in me, and mine
> in her; we are two bodies, but one soul; the union
> between us is like that of the ... heart and the lungs;
> she is my heart, and I am her lungs; but as by heart
> we here understand love, and by lungs wisdom, she
> is the love of my wisdom, and I am the wisdom of
> her love; wherefore her love from without veils my
> wisdom, and my wisdom from within is interiorly
> in her love; hence, as you said, there is an appearance of the unity of our souls in our faces." ... After
> this I looked around, and I saw their tent as overlaid
> with gold, and I asked, "Whence is this?" He replied,
> "It is from a flaming light, which glitters like gold,
> irradiates and tinges the curtains of our tent, whilst
> we are in discourse concerning conjugial love; for
> the heat from our sun, which in its essence is love,
> then bares itself, and tinges the light, which in its
> essence is wisdom, with its own color, which is
> golden; and this takes place because conjugial love,
> in its origin, is the sport of wisdom and love, for the
> man was born to be wisdom, and the woman to be
> the love of the man's wisdom; thence are the delights
> of that sport in conjugial love and from it, between

us and our wives. We have here seen clearly for thousands of years, that those delights as to quantity, degree, and virtue, are excellent and eminent accord - ing to the worship of the Lord Jehovah with us, from Whom that heavenly union, or that heavenly marriage, which is of love and wisdom flows in." As he spoke these words, I saw a great light upon the hill in the midst among the tents, and I asked, "Whence is that light?" And he said, "It is from the sanctuary of the tent of our worship." And I asked whether it was permitted to approach. And he said that it was permitted; and I approached, and saw the tent without and within, altogether according to the description of the tabernacle which was built for the sons; of Israel in the desert, the form whereof was shown to Moses upon Mount Sinai. And I asked, "What is within in that sanctuary, whence there is so great a light?" And he replied, "It is a tablet with this inscription, The Covenant between Jehovah and the Heavens." He said no more. (*Conjugial Love* §75)

"The Covenant between Jehovah and the heavens" is the light of their sanctuary and the light of their lives. Their principle of marriage is that its delights are excellent according as they lay down their own lives and live from the Lord, from whom true marriage comes. A golden principle, truly! Soft from love, and colored with the light of love; pure and bright, and less liable to corruption than principles of any other kind.

The streets of the Holy City, New Jerusalem, are such golden ways of useful life from the Lord—ways of which we know little as yet, but which nevertheless are before us, waiting for us to walk in them. "If a man love Me, he will keep My words; and My Father will love him, and we will come unto him, and make our abode with him," is the golden substance of these heavenly ways.

A practical knowledge of the goodness of the Lord in our uses done from Him is golden coin, stamped with the image of our King; and acknowledgments of His goodness and of our love and duty to Him are ornaments of gold, which we delight to use in His honor.

Silver

THE ANGELS OF THE SILVER AGE* SAID OF THEMSELVES:

> We were from a people in Asia, and the study of our age was the study of truths, by which we had intelligence; this study was the study of our souls and minds; but the study of our bodily senses was the representations of truths in forms; and a knowledge of correspondences conjoined the sensuals of our bodies with the perceptions of our minds, and gained for us intelligence.

In relation to their marriages, they said:

> There is a correspondence between spiritual mar - riage, which is of truth with good, and natural mar -

* The period from Noah until the Tower of Babel.

riage, which is of a man with one wife; and, as we have studied correspondences, we have seen that the Church, with its truths and goods, can by no means be given but with those who live in love truly conjugial with one wife; for the marriage of good and truth is the Church with man; wherefore all here say, that the husband is truth and his wife is good, and that good cannot love any truth but its own, neither can truth in return love any good but its own; if any other were loved, internal marriage, which makes the Church, would perish, and there would be only external marriage, to which idolatry, and not the Church corresponds; therefore mar - riage with one wife we call sacredness; whereas, if it should take place with more than one among us, we should call it sacrilege. (*Conjugial Love* §76)

And then they showed various images and devices, representative of spiritual qualities; and there was presented to them a rainbow which by its flowing colors exhibited the interchange of love and wisdom between husband and wife, all of which things they delighted in, and explained most intelligently.

The principles of spiritual life which are learned through the correspondences of the good things in nature, and especially of the functions in the human body, principles which teach in perfection the duties of charity or neighborly love, are represented by silver. Both harder than gold and whiter, it corresponds to the laws of intelligent spiritual life, a life of spiritual uses to the neighbor. Coins of silver and ornaments are the practical knowledge and acknowledgment of the goodness of such principles, which they have who, by living them, make them their own.

Copper

THE ANGELS FROM THE NEXT AGE, WHICH WAS NAMED from copper,* related:

> We possess, preserved among us, precepts con-
> cerning marriages, from the primeval or most
> ancient people, who were in love truly conjugial...
> while in the world, and are now in a most blessed
> state in their own heaven, which is in the east. We
> are their posterity, and they, as fathers, have given
> us, as their sons, canons of life, among which is this
> concerning marriages: "Sons, if you wish to love
> God and your neighbor, and if you wish to grow
> wise and be happy to eternity, we counsel you to
> live married to one wife; if you recede from this pre -
> cept, every heavenly love will fly from you, and there-
> with internal wisdom, and you will be extermi-
> nated." This precept of our fathers we have obeyed
> as sons, and have perceived its truth, which is, that
> so far as anyone loves his consort alone, he becomes
> heavenly and internal; and that so far as anyone
> does not love his consort alone, he becomes natural
> and external; and this man loves nothing but him-
> self and the images of his own mind, and is mad
> and foolish. From these things it is that we all, in this
> heaven, live married to one wife. (*Conjugial Love* §77)

And afterward they exhibited the collections of precepts
from the most ancient people, by which they were guided

---

* The time from the Tower of Babel until Moses received the
Ten Commandments.

in all their duties. It will be observed that these precepts were given by the people of the Golden Age, among whom they were golden precepts. Received by those who live them not intelligently, or from the perception of love, but obediently, from a desire for the promised reward, they become copper. Much of the light is left out; a keen scent detects in them the odor of selfishness, unperceived by their possessors, who are not in interior perception; and because of the lack of interior humility and purity in which the Lord can dwell immediately, they are sadly liable to corrosion by the allurements of what seems pleasant and good. (See the Note on the Copper and Iron Ages at the end of the volume.)

Iron

Again we descend to principles of a still lower kind, and are instructed by those who are in them concerning their marriages:

> We do not live with one wife, but some with two and three, and some with more, because variety, obedience, and honor, as of majesty, delight us; and these we have from our wives, if they are many; with one wife there would be no pleasure from variety, but disgust from sameness; nor flattering courteousness from obedience, but disquietude from equality; nor satisfaction from dominion and honor thence, but vexation from disputes concerning superiority. And what is a woman? Is she not born subject to the will of the man? To serve and not to rule?

Wherefore here every husband in his own house has, as it were, royal majesty; and because this is of our love, it is also the blessedness of our life.

After some reproofs by Swedenborg for the selfishness of their love:

There appeared through the gate, as it were, lightning; and I asked, "What is this?" He said, "Such lightning is to us a sign that there will come the Ancient one from the East, who teaches us concerning God, that He is one, alone; Omnipotent, Who is the first and the last; He also admonishes us not to worship idols, but only to look at them as images representative of the virtues proceeding from the one God, which together form His worship. This Ancient one is our angel, whom we revere, and to whom we hearken; he comes to us, and raises us up, when we are falling into obscure worship of God, from fantasy respecting images." (*Conjugial Love* §78)

As the knowledge of the Lord's love became with the men of the Copper Age mere precepts of natural good, so the intelligent love of spiritual truth and of representative forms in the Silver Age becomes with these last mere worship of idols, and obedience to iron laws which forbid evil, and prescribe penalties for disobedience. The kindly softness, the brightness, and the resistance to corruption of the Silver Age are gone. We have left only the truth that is essential to existence, necessarily hard, inflexible, and peremptory, because beyond that is destruction. Low as it is, compared with silver and gold, it is truth which the

Christian world has mixed with the clay of artificial and arbitrary teachings of goodness and truth. But it is again asserting itself, breaking off the weak clay, and laying a foundation, at least genuine and natural, for better principles. It is moral, civil, and natural law, by which the community is protected from injury; it is law that compels everyone to be fair in his dealings, truthful, honest, faithful, and orderly, if from no better motive, from fear of evil consequences to himself. The penal laws of society are applications of such principles. And whenever, from change of circumstances or states, a form of law becomes unsuitable, the principle of the law can be recast in another form.

Carbon

AN IMPORTANT ELEMENT IN THE AIR AND THE EARTH IS carbonic acid, the carbon of which, separated from the oxygen by plant life, constitutes the main part of the substance of wood, and hence, also, of coal. It is the solid element in starch, sugar, and fat, and furnishes the fat-making and heat-giving food for the body. Carbon is found, also, in the form of plumbago, or black lead, and in that of diamonds. Carbon does not contain heat in itself, and is not in itself a source of heat; but during the process of separating the carbon from the carbonic acid absorbed in the sap of the plant, so that it may be deposited in fruit or grain or woody fiber, a portion of the sun's heat is absorbed and expended, equal to the heat again evolved by the reuniting of oxygen with the carbon, in combustion either by fire or by the slow processes of animal life or of decay.

No work or effort either of thought or of production is possible but under the stimulus of some affection, and all affection comes either directly or indirectly from the Lord, Who is the only Source of affection. And in the same way, no growth or production is possible in plants, but under the stimulus of heat, which comes either directly or indirectly from the sun. The deposit of carbon is the chief result of this stimulus in plants, and seems to correspond to the experience or the fact of the reception and enjoyment of affection from the Lord during the human processes of thinking and working which correspond to the growth and fruitfulness of plants.

The practical religious life of mankind, in ages when the Lord is known and loved, is composed mostly of such experience; and this is laid up as habits and traditions of trust in God, and belief in life from God, which sustain some degree of spiritual life and activity in times and ages when there is no direct knowledge of God and reception from Him. They are like deposits of wood from the summer to be used in the winter, and deposits of coal in the youthful days of the world, to be drawn upon during the slow process of coming into a rational understanding of the Lord and full relations of manly love to Him.

The religious life of today is sustained by such habits and traditions from the early Christian Church, and from still earlier Churches, though there is almost no sense of spiritual warmth and enlightenment directly from the Lord; and a truly rational knowledge of the Lord is only in its first beginning. And this is parallel to the dependence of the world upon the deposits of coal from the days of the youth of the world, which now furnishes the working power for their machinery (which is a sort of material rationality), while they are learning to obtain a full supply of energy directly from the sun.

Plumbago, which is a non-combustible mineral deposit of the same material, seems to represent a historical knowledge of natural benefits from the Lord, such as appears in the story of the Jews. It is interesting that it should be combined with clay (which stands for the current knowledge of natural fact) to make lead pencils, for record of current impressions; and also that it is used for the blacking of stoves, and other iron implements used for the control of fire—as if to add to the natural laws by which such control is exercised, a recognition of the source of the activity that is controlled, and of the power that controls it.

The diamond, the hardest and most brilliant of precious stones, stands for the spiritual fact that all love, or life, is from the Lord. No other gem so perfectly reflects the light of the sun; and no other truth so absolutely ascribes all to the Lord, retaining so little to self.

Sulphur

SULPHUR OCCURS AS A COMMON MINERAL IN VOLCANIC countries, also in combination with other minerals as sulphides and sulphates everywhere. It is an essential element of albumen, and of albuminous, or muscle-making articles of food; also of all tissues of the body. Though a mineral, it is extremely combustible, burning with a blue flame which gives little light but great heat. The products of the combustion are sulphurous and sulphuric acids, both intensely corrosive destroyers of plant and animal tissues.

All minerals correspond to fact or law; and this apparently mineral substance, yet so combustible and volatile, seems to have its correspondence with what we may be permitted to call the fact of man's voluntary *proprium*; that is, the fact that man's life is his own, and that he himself determines the activities of his life. This seems like a fact, and all the fire of self-love is bound up in it, and burns hotly and angrily when the real truth of the apparent fact is exposed. The real truth is that man has no life of his own, but lives from the Lord, and that the Lord gives to man the consciousness of living of himself, that he may as of himself do the good things which the Lord commands, and enjoy the Lord's love of doing them. Yet the apparent fact is essential to man's freedom, and to his existence as man; just as essential as sulphur is to all the tissues of his body. But when the apparent fact is confirmed as the real truth, and man determines not to live as of himself in doing the Lord's will, but to live absolutely of himself according to what seems good to him, then this apparent fact becomes the basis of the love of self, and all the evil lusts of self-love come forth from it. The effect of thought from self-love in destroying the happiness of others, as described in *Heaven and Hell* §399, is much like that of the fumes of sulphur in suffocating all living beings and corroding their tissues. They also quickly tarnish and corrode all metals but the noblest. On this account fire and brimstone are used in the Word to typify the heat and lustfulness of the wicked in hell; and "the lusts of evil" is the meaning given by Swedenborg. Yet in its necessary presence in the composition of the body, and its occurrence in the earth in stony form, we see a correspondence with the necessary apparent fact that man lives of himself; from the confirmation of which the lusts of evil spring forth.

Phosphorous

A SUBSTANCE VERY SIMILAR TO SULPHUR IN SOME RESPECTS is phosphorus. It too is a mineral, but so very inflammable that it never occurs in an uncombined mineral form. It burns with an intense white flame. It is necessary and abundant in animal tissues, especially those of the brain and nerves, and of the bones. Our supply of phosphorus as a mineral is obtained from bones.

The similarity of this substance to sulphur, together with its necessary presence in the brain, and the bright light with which it burns, suggests its correspondence with what we may call the fact of the intellectual *proprium* of man; that is, the apparent truth that we think and reason and discern of ourselves. Perhaps this is not thought of as a fact because it never is called in question. That we think of ourselves is no more questioned, or thought of, than that we are. "I think; therefore I am," is the basis of modern philosophy. And yet the truth is that the Lord gives both the faculty and the light by which we think and discern; and the appearance, also, that the faculty is our own, in order that we may as of ourselves think the truth which He loves to think, and which is the guide to all goodness. We cannot think at all without this appearance; it is necessary to any mental activity; yet if we confirm it as the truth, we surrender ourselves to the guidance of every will-o'-the-wisp which our brains may send forth of themselves.

The bones, also, are depositories of phosphorus, because bones are correspondences of the truths formulated and fixed in the memory and the life, which give form and support to all thought and action; and the formulating and fixing of such truths is done as of ourselves, by our own intellectual choice and act.

The Sunbeam

When a sunbeam passes through a prism of glass or salt or water or other transparent material, it is separated into elements of different qualities. Some of these elements we see in the rainbow colors of the spectrum; others are invisible, but can be detected by suitable instruments. The sunbeam is separated in this way by being turned out of its direct course, some of its elements being more easily bent than others. Of the pencils of light which form the rainbow colors, the red is bent least and the violet most; the orange, yellow, green, and blue arranging themselves in order between the extremes according to their degrees of flexibility. But there is a pencil of invisible rays, which the thermometer shows to be rays of heat, which is turned from its course still less than the red, and makes an invisible extension of the spectrum, as of a color too red to be seen; and there is another portion of rays that is bent more than the violet and extends the spectrum invisibly at the other end—which rays affect the photographic plate and produce other chemical changes, on account of which they are often called "chemical rays." The heat rays are very sensible beyond the red, but extend also perceptibly through the whole or nearly the whole visible spectrum. The chemical rays are not so well known, but it is enough for our present purpose to know that those which make the photograph are most intense in the pale violet region; that beyond these they are active, and, though ordinarily invisible, can be made visible by bodies that are phosphorescent or fluorescent; and that chemical effects are produced in other substances by the rays of other parts of the spectrum, those changes that are essential to vegetable growth taking place most rapidly in the yellow light.

All these effects of heat, light, and chemical power are produced by active motions of various kinds in the ether; the motions that produce any given effect being necessarily uniform and constant, though exceedingly complex and rapid. So uniform are the movements that produce light, that their size and rapidity can be exactly determined and are always the same in the same color. In the red color of the spectrum, it is said that 39,000 motions succeed one another in a single inch, and their motion is propagated with such incredible quickness that more than 470 millions of millions of them affect the eye in a single second. Of the violet motions 57,500 are required to fill an inch, and 699 millions of millions impinge upon the eye in a second. The heat motions affect larger masses of the ether, rolling it, as it were, in larger waves, fewer of which are contained in a given space, or will strike the body in a given time. "The ethers and airs made active in masses produce heat, but modified in particulars they produce light." The same is said of the spiritual atmospheres, as to their effects in the spiritual world: "Made active in generals they give heat, and modified in particulars they give light" (*Apocalypse Explained* §726). But at the other end of the spectrum, the motions of the chemical rays are still more minute and more rapid than those of violet light.

And what does the sunbeam accomplish with this intense and varied vitality? Imagine the earth deprived of the rays of the sun. If we can think of it as existing at all, we have a dead earth; the waters are hard and still as rock; the air itself is frozen to a case of stone; vegetable and animal life are gone; even mineral life is suspended; darkness, cold, and death prevail everywhere. Admit the sunbeams again, and the winds move, the waters flow and dance, the crystals busily pile their tiny masses, and verdure begins to clothe the earth, and to give nourishment to animals.

In a physical sense, the sunbeam gives life to the world; and, in the same physical sense, it is the creator of the world; that is, it is the natural means by which the Lord animates and forms the world.

It is heat which is the life of the world, and it is light with its peculiar invisible extension of chemical power, which enables it to take form (*Apocalypse Explained* §1206). Consider the part which light performs in the growth of plants.

Heat and moisture are sufficient to put in motion the substance of a seed or bulb; but cut off light from it entirely, and if there is not mere decay, and no growing form at all, the growth is at best only a feeble development of the materials for growth already laid up in the seed; there is no new material formed. Bring the seed to the light, and its pale, sickly expansion stops; it assimilates new food from the air and the earth; it spreads forth and multiplies new leaves tinged with healthy green and full of veins and pores and little vessels for useful work. It produces flowers of bright, glad colors, expressive of delight in the good work it can now accomplish; and finally perfects its seed or fruit which it offers for the food of men and beasts. How the light builds up those marvelous forms we do not fully know. But it seems that the activity of its own particulars it communicates to the substances of the plant and to the materials which serve for its food, and the plant life avails itself of so much of that motion as is needful to effect the chemical and other modifications that belong to its growth. So that the forms of the growth of the plant are a part of the forms of motion of the light, made visible and interpreted to us.

The heat-giving power which the plant has when burnt or consumed as food is also the heat of the sunshine temporarily fixed and stored. And apparently all its physical properties and powers are those of the sunshine, interpreted to us according to the nature of the plant.

Swedenborg says:

> The sun of heaven is the Lord, the light there is Divine Truth, and the heat there is Divine Good, which proceed from the Lord as a sun. It is from that origin that all things proceed which exist and appear in heaven. (*Heaven and Hell* §117)

And further:

> How immense, and of what nature, the Divine Love is, may be inferred from a comparison with the sun of this world. It is most ardent; and, if you will believe it, it is much more ardent than this. (*Heaven and Hell* §120)

A glorious image, indeed, is the sun, even as we see it, with our present limited knowledge, its intense heat permeating the solar system, giving life and activity to every particle in it, which moves as if of its own energy, yet altogether from the sun; its light building everywhere beautiful natural forms, which seem to grow of themselves, yet can do nothing but with the forming activity of the light. A glorious image it is, and more glorious for every gain of knowledge about it, of that heavenly Sunbeam by which is everything heavenly made that is made, whose heat is the Divine Love, which gives every human mind the faculty of living and loving as of itself, yet always and only from the Lord, and whose light is the wisdom which gives form to every human thought and plan and purpose, in beauty and excellence according to the degree of wisdom which the mind receives, the man all the while seeming to think and plan and speak altogether from himself.

That love and wisdom are the heat and light of the mind is evident to the senses in the spiritual world; for "all celestial and spiritual heat, or love and charity, are perceived in an external form in heaven as something flamy from the sun, and all celestial and spiritual light. . . appears in an external form in heaven as light from the sun. . . . All good is from the heat which flows from the Lord as a sun, and all truth is from the light thence; and, further, all affections which are of love or good, are variations of that celestial and spiritual heat which is from the Lord, and thence are changes of state; and all thoughts which are of faith or truth, are variegations of that celestial and spiritual light which is from the Lord, and thence is intelligence. In this heat and light are all the angels who are in heaven, and their affections and thoughts are from no other source, and are nothing else" (*Arcana Coelestia* §3862).

Colors

THE LIGHT WHICH PROCEEDS FROM THE LORD PURE, HOMO-geneous, and apparently simple in quality is received variously by the angels; no two are in exactly the same degree and quality of wisdom and, therefore, no two are in light of precisely the same degree and color. From the very light about an angel another angel perceives instantly the quality of the wisdom and intelligence within him. The angels, also, can discourse together, expressing their thoughts with the utmost fullness and distinctness, merely by variations of light and color; the meaning of which is instantly perceived.

If we were in the spiritual world, and were to receive flowers of beautiful colors—crimson, scarlet, white, yellow, and blue, with variations and mixtures of them—from the affection that flowed in as we looked at them we should know instantly the correspondence and origin of the colors. The same affection flows in as we look at them here, and produces the pleasant glow of heart which makes us love the colors; but we are too obtuse to perceive the quality of the affections. Still, if we attend to the correspondence as Swedenborg teaches it to us, we shall find many things from reason and from our own perceptions to confirm it.

Swedenborg says that there are two general colors, red and white, and that "the other colors, as green, yellow, blue, and many more are composed of them," modified by black (*Apocalypse Revealed* §915). This is evidently true of many colors; but we are in the habit of thinking of yellow and blue as pure, simple colors. Yellow is, however, white warmed by a red which is inseparable from it. Why it is inseparable we shall see presently. A decided blue is made by the mixture of white and black; or, better, by a thin layer of white over a black ground, as in black onyx. This seems to be the cause of the blueness of wood smoke. Seen against the sky, it is of a dirty white color; but against a background of dark green and shadow, it is blue. Not very beautiful blues are made in this way by our pigments; yet there seems to be no other color needed to produce them, only a more perfect blending of these.

Crimson, scarlet, and yellow are warm colors; white and blue are cool colors.

We call red "warm," from a perception that it is from fire, and that it is expressive of some glowing affection. And we call blue "cool" from its association with water and the sky, and from a perception of quiet purity and absence of passion in it. And this is as far as we usually go in our discrimination of colors. Swedenborg says that the warmest red, the pure crimson of the finest rubies, is the color of that deepest human love—love to the Lord. This is the deepest and warmest love because it is nearest to Him Who is the Sun of the Heavens, and the Source of all heavenly heat and love; and when such love is presented to the sight in heaven it is through the ruby color. It is this color that Swedenborg means by purple, which he always says represents "celestial love," or love to the Lord (*Arcana Coelestia* §9467; *True Christian Religion* §216).

They who love the Lord, love also what is from Him in one another. Therefore from love to the Lord proceeds mutual love (*Arcana Coelestia* §9468), less deep and warm, perhaps, but more evident to the senses; and when this love is represented by light, it appears of a scarlet hue; a color less deeply red but brighter than the ruby (*Apocalypse Revealed* §725). When this same love desires to put itself forth in good works for the neighbor from the Lord, it gathers to itself still more of light and presents itself in the color of the brightest part of the spectrum, golden yellow. It is because this is the color of uses done from love to the Lord that fields of ripening grain, especially wheat, which represents duties done from the Lord, are yellow;

oranges, also, which represent the wisdom of conjugial love; and gold of which the streets of the Holy City, that is the ways of life for those who know and love the Lord, are made; and the oil of olives, which are the fruits of those who love to perceive the merciful goodness of the Lord. And now we see why the red cannot be separated from the white in yellow. It is because it is the color of works done, in which love and wisdom are inseparably united. Therefore also, when angels are in discourse concerning conjugial love, a golden light plays about them (*Conjugial Love* §75), which they say is from the heat of their sun united with its light; and some in the world of spirits, when they are in meditation concerning conjugial love, see golden rain falling from heaven (*Conjugial Love* §155, 208).

White light is light with the warmth left out. It corresponds to wisdom in states in which the love within it is not felt. It is the light of the moon, or of states of faith in which the Lord's love is not perceived. It is the light reflected from silver, from the diamond, from clouds, and from snow, which represent respectively various forms of pure truth (*True Christian Religion* §216). It is also the general color of light, not discriminated into colors; and is the light of those who are in general truths (*Apocalypse Revealed* §566).

The blue of the sky is produced by the blending of the white light reflected by the atmosphere with the black which would be the color of the sky were there no air. It is said that the air itself is slightly blue. If this be so, no doubt it adds to the beauty of the color of the sky, which would, however, be blue if the air were entirely white. Blackness represents the want of spiritual light, that is a state of utter spiritual ignorance, such as is the state of every man before regeneration begins, and such as every spiritual man knows and confesses his own state to be without illumination from the Lord. But when that confession of darkness is illumined by the light of wisdom from the Lord, it presents itself to view in the heavens as a sky blue color; which color therefore represents a state of spiritual enlightenment, and of affection for pure truth.

This beautiful blue appears in nature chiefly in the sky, and in large bodies of water which reflect the blue of the sky. Both the air and the water correspond to purifying truth which teaches what is right and wrong, good and evil; the water representing such truth concerning works, and the air concerning thoughts and feelings.

When this truth is applied to our relation to the Lord, with the effort to do justice to the Lord from the fire of love to Him, there appears another beautiful color which Swedenborg calls "hyacinthine blue," that is, blue permeated with ruby red, and which he explains as the color of truth from love to the Lord (*Arcana Coelestia* §9466; *True Christian Religion* §220).

The many purples that are composed of shades of blue and red combined are to be understood in the same way, as the colors of intelligent love of truth from various kinds of warm affection, according to the quality of the red.

Green is composed of blue combined with yellow. It is the general color of foliage, prevailing everywhere in nature, all over the surface of the earth. Now, blue is the color of the love of truth, and yellow is the color of good works, which are spiritual grains and fruits. Green, therefore, represents the love of truth for the sake of uses. And what are green leaves? The leaves are the part of a plant that receives the water drawn up by the roots, with the nourishment it contains, and exposes it to the air and sunlight, throwing out what is superfluous, and absorbing from both air and sunshine elements which it combines with the sap to make the substance of wood and fruit, which it returns to the tree. The leaves correspond evidently to the faculty of perceiving truth for the sake of use, and of course are green in color.

Now, then, let us return to the spectrum, remembering that the spectrum shows the elements of the sunbeam in the order in which they are turned from their direct course by all transparent substances of suitable form. And first we have invisible rays of heat, least of all bent from the direct line in which the sun sends them; an image and outbirth of the Lord's love affecting insensibly, yet being the life of, the inmost part of the human spirit. We may not be wrong in thinking that we have here a correspondence of the reception of the Lord in those unconscious inmosts of human minds, which taken together compose what Swedenborg calls "the heaven of human internals" (*Arcana Coelestia* §1999). The crimson red comes first to view; the color of first consciousness of the Lord's love, and of love for Him in turn. The red, brightening through various shades, gives place to yellow; as love to the Lord, gathering its appropriate wisdom, leads to uses from the Lord.

A little more deflected we see the green; an obscurer perception of truth, yet still for the sake of doing good. Then the clear, cool blue of affection for spiritual truth, deepening according to the diminishing intelligence of the recipients through darker blues. And, closing the visible spectrum, we have a deep violet, in the blush of which there is an assurance that truth from the Lord both begins and ends in love. And, finally, we have the so-called chemical rays, extending beyond the rays of light and of heat, with power to affect the order and arrangement of particles corresponding to the power of the Divine truth to keep in order and to arrange for uses beings that have no consciousness of receiving life from the Lord.

As, therefore, the sunbeam is a representative and ultimate form of the Divine love and wisdom, continually forming and vivifying the souls of men with their own goodness and truth, so the rainbow, which is the natural form of the spectrum, is a representative and ultimate form of the varied reception of that love and wisdom by men. It is called "a token of the covenant between God and men"; for it is a natural representative of the communication of heavenly goodness and truth by the Lord and the reception of them by men; and this communication and reception are the two parts of the covenant by virtue of which men are saved and enjoy eternal life (*Apocalypse Explained* §595).

In the heavens rainbows appear, not always with a regular series of colors as in ours, sometimes of one color only, and the color corresponding with the affection of the angels present (*Arcana Coelestia* §1042). In the highest heaven there appear rainbows of a beautiful ruby color, because the angels there are in love to the Lord, and in full perception of His love; in the middle heaven of brilliant blue, because the angels of it are in the delight of receiving wisdom from the Lord; and in the lowest heaven of emerald green with angels who are in the love of good but in obscure perception of truth, or of white, with those who are in general or common spiritual truth (*Apocalypse Revealed* §232, 566; *Apocalypse Explained* §269).

In the natural world our particular states are not represented around us. We are not here to enjoy the full development of any state of goodness or truth, but to choose, among all possible states of good or evil, that which we will make our own. The natural objects of this world are, therefore, representatives of all spiritual states presented in a general form; and we choose among them those that we like. If our tastes are natural and simple—not artificial or hypocritical—we are delighted with the things that agree with our spiritual states; they open the senses and the natural mind to the inflow of the affections which delight our souls; and these flow down then into the sense as into open vessels, with gentle thrills of pleasure. This is the cause of our interior delight in the bright colors of flowers, in the beauty of the rainbow, in the blue sky and brilliant clouds, and especially of our restful, expansive satisfaction in the warm, creative light of the returning spring. An innocent, peaceful delight flows into all these things from heaven; and the affections from which it comes are the heavenly things to which the natural correspond.

Creation through the Sun

ANOTHER SERIES OF FACTS IS DISCLOSED TO US BY THE solar spectrum. When a solid or a liquid is white hot, it gives a spectrum which shows all the bands of color continuously. But a shining hot vapor, as of a burning candle, or any burning metal, gives only bars of color; and every substance has its own bars or series of bars. When the light from the incandescent, solid passes through the shining vapor, instead of increasing the intensity of the parts of the spectrum answering to its own bars, the vapor puts them out; so that the spectrum is interrupted by dark bars. Now the spectrum of the sun, when examined with appropriate glasses, shows a multitude of such dark bars, many of which answer to the bars of well-known metals and gases which enter into the composition of the earth and its atmospheres. And this seems to prove that incandescent vapors of those substances exist between the more solid part of the sun and us—probably in the immediate atmosphere of the sun. The telescope reveals to us the fact that the sun is surrounded with masses of such vapor shooting up from its surface like immense flames, and sometimes with a velocity of many thousand miles in a minute. The dark spots often seen upon the sun are openings in the flamy atmosphere, disclosing the relatively darker, but still bright, mass beneath. The spots are most extensive when the activity of the flames is greatest, and indeed they seem to be caused by that activity. And it is remarkable that in the moments of most intense activity, the magnetic needles all over our earth are agitated; and where it is night, auroral flashes are displayed. And one thing more should be added, which is that a fine dust, composed of some at least of such elements as are detected in the flamy masses about the sun, is constantly falling upon the earth. It is known by the name of the "cosmic dust," and probably adds some hundreds of tons to the mass of the earth every year.

We are taught in the revelations given to the New Church that there is a creative influence proceeding from the Lord, which appears as the sun in heaven; and that from that sun proceed atmospheres which furnish the means of all creations in the spiritual world, which all are animated by the love and the wisdom of the Lord. We are taught that these atmospheres descend and become grosser by discrete degrees, or steps, until the last plane of spiritual life is reached; and that the next step is from the last spiritual to the first and purest natural, which is not in itself living from the love of the Lord, but is the perfect instrument of that love in creating and actuating the natural world. That purest natural substance is the fire of the natural sun or suns, which is the first natural embodiment of the Divine desire to create earths from which men may rise with the capacity to know and love God. This fire, intensely active, sends forth from itself the elements of which worlds are made; first the purer atmospheres—the aura which is the means of binding all things to itself and to their uses, by the forces which we call gravity and cohesion; and the ether which is the means of animating and modifying all the otherwise inert materials, by the forces of heat, light, and probably electricity and magnetism. Then follow the elements of the air, and those other elements, at first in the form of fiery vapors, from which come earths and metals.

As to these things the sun is a correspondence and an expression of the Lord's creative love. His love is a love of giving Himself to men who can receive and be blessed by it. He puts Himself forth in the spiritual sun; and in the natural sun He puts forth all the elements of Himself in their ultimate forms, all of which forms are from Himself as Man, corresponding to the elements of man, and capable of being built into man. The correspondence of some of the elements of the earth with man we have already seen; the correspondence of them all could be traced, no doubt, by patient study. They all come from the sun, and many of them can be distinctly discovered in the atmosphere of the sun, because the sun is the means by which God creates from Himself beings who can receive His own life; and God is a Divine Man.

THE ATMOSPHERES

THERE ARE ATMOSPHERES PROCEEDING FROM THE SUN OF heaven, corresponding to the planes of the heavens. In the grossest of them, which seems almost watery to the angels above, dwell the angels of the lowest heaven; in a distinctly or discretely purer atmosphere dwell the angels of the higher heaven; and in an exquisitely pure air dwell the angels of the highest heaven. There are, no doubt, degrees within these degrees, and degrees above them in which the unconscious internals of man reside; but this is the usual statement, and is sufficiently full for our purpose.

To these general divisions of the spiritual atmospheres, the three natural atmospheres—the aura, the ether, and the air—correspond; the aura to the sphere of love from the Lord to the Lord and the neighbor, which fills the inmost heaven, and through that pervades all the heavens, and binds them to the Lord and to one another; to this also the brain and nervous system in the human body correspond. The ether has relation to the sphere of intelligent love which pervades the middle heaven, and through it gives guidance and impulses of charity to the lower heavens; corresponding to the uses of the heart and the lungs to the limbs and muscular and bony systems in the body. And the air has relation to the sphere of effects in the lowest heaven, through which the actual operations of development, increase, purification, and protection are performed upon the spirits of men. And therefore the forces of the wind are so often used to represent the action of the spiritual world in the natural. "God formed man of the dust of the ground and breathed into his nostrils the breath of life." The Lord breathed on His disciples, and said, "Receive ye the Holy Spirit." "Come from the four winds, O breath, and breathe into these slain, that they may live" (Ezekiel 37:10). (See *Apocalypse Revealed* §343.)

The elements of these atmospheres are not so simple as might at first be supposed. We know little of the composition of the ether and the aura, but more about that of the air. The principal elements of the air are nitrogen and oxygen; but other constant elements are hydrogen, and various compounds of these three with one another such as watery vapor and ammonia; and also very many compounds with carbon, the chief of which is carbonic acid gas, but among which also would be included a large part of the vapors of essential oils, which make the perfumes of flowers, also most of the exhalations of plants and animals; compounds of hydrogen and of oxygen with sulphur also, and possibly with many other substances. Everything exhales from itself a sphere of its own substance, which is like an odor about it. Many metals, even, can be recognized by the odor of their spheres. And yet chemistry cannot detect the presence of the substance in the air; and possibly the particles exhaled do not belong to the air, but to the purer atmosphere which we have called ether. There is an immense amount of exhalations contained in the atmospheres, some of them healthful and some noxious; also a multitude of living germs, animal or vegetable, which produce ferments and molds.

Oxygen

THE OXYGEN AND THE NITROGEN MAY BE CONSIDERED AS the chief elements of the air, and other things as dependent upon circumstances. Oxygen, or the acid maker, has its name from its capacity for uniting with other substances and making acids of them. Its faculty seems to be that of making active what otherwise is inert, or of developing the proper quality and capacity of other substances. Of hydrogen it makes water; of nitrogen various oxides and potent acids; of sulphur some of the most powerful acids; of carbon, phosphorus, arsenic, iron, and many other metals, active acids, each with its own properties. With most of these an effect of union with oxygen is to produce the heat and light which we associate with combustion.

If this is a just view of the properties of oxygen, its correspondence seems to be with an atmosphere of pure truth from the Lord, which brings out the real qualities of things, and shows them just as they are.

Nitrogen

NITROGEN, ON THE CONTRARY, BY ITS INERTNESS DILUTES the oxygen, and prevents it from too rapidly dissolving organic combinations, and reducing everything to its elementary condition. It seems to have no love for combining with oxygen, being mixed with it in the air for an indefinite time without union in any degree. By various organic processes it is combined with oxygen, hydrogen, carbon, and a little sulphur, of which elements all tissues and muscles in animal bodies are composed; also the grains and other nitrogenized kinds of food, by which such tissues are nourished. From the decomposition of such compounds, other compounds of nitrogen exist, as ammonia, nitrous and nitric acids, saltpeter, which is nitric acid and potash, and the numerous explosives which are made of nitric acid with carbon compounds. The power of these seems to arise from the quantity of oxygen lightly held by the nitrogen, and set free by heat or a blow to unite with other substances.

The correspondence of nitrogen seems to be with the atmosphere of protection and accommodation from the Lord; or, if a more positive form of statement is preferred, to the truth that all men are at liberty to accommodate the absolute truth to themselves; by means of which they can think apparent truth, or a little truth, as they are able to bear it, and their thoughts are not too rapidly disintegrated before they have done their use. Everyone's present theories, plans, views, states of feeling, will be disintegrated in time, reduced to their elements of fact, and give place to others; as the tissues of every plant and animal will be reduced to their simple elements by oxidation, and give place to others. And this would be done suddenly and at once, if everyone was compelled to think the pure truth, unaccommodated; just as would happen with the corresponding natural phenomena in an atmosphere of pure oxygen. The liberty of accommodating truth to himself everyone must take to himself, and from it everyone must act, or he would not be himself and have any power at all to act. And therefore it is that nitrogen is an essential element of muscular and other tissues which make man and every animal to be himself, with power to act of himself.

But the truth that is thus held in restraint by man's liberty of accommodating it to himself does not lose its force, even though restrained by custom long after the living power that bound it has disappeared from the scene; and upon occasions of violent feeling, or other emergency, it may assert itself with tremendous force. Our chief explosives, gunpowder, gun cotton, dynamite, and others, all owe their power to the oxygen held in restraint by nitrogen.

The Air in General

THESE PRINCIPAL AND CONSTANT ELEMENTS OF THE AIR, together with other elements proceeding directly from the sun, correspond to and are the ultimates of the general sphere proceeding from the Lord through the heavens for the uses of creation and preservation. The exhalations and odors that proceed from all created things and mingle with these general elements correspond to the spheres of thought and affection that proceed from angels and spirits and men upon the earth; of which Swedenborg has very much to tell us. The breathing of pure air, which purifies and stimulates the blood, corresponds with the thinking of pure truth, adapted to our state, and the purification of our affections by it. The breathing of sweet and nourishing odors and exhalations corresponds to the perception and enjoyment of spheres of spiritual affection and thought from others. And the breathing of foul odors corresponds to the reception of a sphere of foul and contaminating thought and feeling. We recognize this in familiar speech when we speak of good and bad moral atmospheres.[1]

1. On the correspondence of various odors and stenches, see *True Christian Religion* §569, 570; *Divine Providence* §40, 304, 340; *Conjugial Love* §461; *Heaven and Hell* §429, 488; *Arcana Coelestia* §7225; and many other places.

Note on the Copper and Iron Ages

The people of the Copper and the Iron ages, described in the Relations quoted, all lived before the Coming of the Lord; only the iron mixed with clay being assigned to the Christian period. But the terms are more relative than absolute, and are variously applied. Swedenborg often disregards the Hebrew Church as separate from that of Israel, and names only the Most Ancient, the Ancient, the Israelitish, and the Christian. And in this classification the Israelitish is copper relatively to the Ancient, and the Christian is iron, and later iron and clay, relatively to the Israelitish. But when the Hebrew is distinguished from the Israelitish as a separate church, then relatively to the Silver Age it is plainly copper, and the Israelitish relatively to the Hebrew is plainly iron.

SPIRITUAL WORKS *by*
EMANUEL SWEDENBORG

SWEDENBORG ORIGINALLY PUBLISHED HIS BOOKS IN LATIN. Throughout the years, these books have been translated into dozens of languages, including various English editions. To find the latest translation, inquire at your favorite bookstore or visit www.swedenborg.com.

APOCALYPSE EXPLAINED
   Modern Title: *Revelation Explained*
   Original Title: *Apocalypsis Explicata secundum Sensum Spiritualem, Ubi Revelantur Arcana, Quae Ibi Praedicta, et Hactenus Recondita Fuerunt* [The Book of Revelation Explained as to Its Spiritual Meaning, Which Reveals Secret Wonders That Were Predicted There and Have Been Hidden until Now].
   London: 1834–1840 (published posthumously).

APOCALYPSE REVEALED
   Modern Title: *Revelation Unveiled*
   Original Title: *Apocalypsis Revelata, in Qua Deteguntur Arcana Quae Ibi Praedicta Sunt, et Hactenus Recondita Latuerunt* [The Book of Revelation Unveiled, Uncovering the Secrets That Were Foretold There and Have Lain Hidden until Now]. Amsterdam: 1766.

ARCANA COELESTIA

Modern Title: *Secrets of Heaven*
Original Title: *Arcana Coelestia, Quae in Scriptura Sacra, seu Verbo Domini Sunt, Detecta: . . . Una cum Mirabilibus Quae Visa Sunt in Mundo Spirituum, etin Coelo Angelorum* [A Disclosure of Secrets of Heaven Contained in Sacred Scripture, or the Word of the Lord, . . . Together with Amazing Things Seen in the World of Spirits and in the Heaven of Angels]. London: 1749–1756.

BRIEF EXPOSITION

Modern Title: *Survey*
Original Title: *Summaria Expositio Doctrinae Novae Ecclesiae, Quae per Novam Hierosolymam in Apocalypsi Intelligitur* [Survey of Teachings for the New Church Meant by the New Jerusalem in the Book of Revelation]. Amsterdam: 1769.

CONJUGIAL LOVE

Modern Title: *Marriage Love*
Original Title: *Delitiae Sapientiae de Amore Conjugiali: Post Quas Sequuntur Voluptates Insaniae de Amore Scortatorio* [Wisdom's Delight in Marriage Love: Followed by Insanity's Pleasure in Promiscuous Love]. Amsterdam: 1768.

CONTINUATION CONCERNING THE LAST JUDGMENT

Modern Title: *Supplements*
Original Title: *Continuatio de Ultimo Judicio: Et de Mundo Spirituali* [Supplements on the Last Judgment and the Spiritual World]. Amsterdam: 1763.

DIVINE LOVE AND WISDOM

Modern Title: *Divine Love and Wisdom*
Original Title: *Sapientia Angelica de Divino Amore et de Divina Sapientia* [Angelic Wisdom about Divine Love and Wisdom]. Amsterdam: 1763.

DIVINE PROVIDENCE

Modern Title: *Divine Providence*
Original Title: *Sapientia Angelica de Divina Providentia* [Angelic Wisdom about Divine Providence]. Amsterdam: 1764.

DOCTRINE OF FAITH

Modern Title: *Faith*
Original Title: *Doctrina Novae Hierosolymae de Fide* [Teachings for the New Jerusalem on Faith]. Amsterdam: 1763.

DOCTRINE OF LIFE

Modern title: *Life*
Original title: *Doctrina Vitae pro Nova Hierosolyma ex Praeceptis Decalogi* [Teachings about Life for the New Jerusalem: Drawn from the Ten Commandments]. Amsterdam: 1763.

DOCTRINE OF THE LORD

Modern Title: *The Lord*
Original Title: *Doctrina Novae Hierosolymae de Domino* [Teachings for the New Jerusalem on the Lord]. Amsterdam: 1763.

DOCTRINE OF THE SACRED SCRIPTURE

Modern title: *Sacred Scripture*

Original title: *Doctrina Novae Hierosolymae de Scriptura Sacra* [Teachings for the New Jerusalem on Sacred Scripture]. Amsterdam: 1763.

EARTHS IN THE UNIVERSE
Modern Title: *Other Planets*
Original Title: *De Telluribus in Mundo Nostro Solari, Quae Vocantur Planetae, et de Telluribus in Coelo Astrifero, deque Illarum Incolis, Tum de Spiritibus et Angelis Ibi: Ex Auditis et Visis* [Planets or Worlds in Our Solar System, and Worlds in the Starry Heavens, and Their Inhabitants, As Well as the Spirits and Angels There: Drawn from Things Heard and Seen]. London: 1758.

HEAVEN AND HELL
Modern Title: *Heaven and Hell*
Original Title: *De Coelo et Ejus Mirabilibus, et de Inferno, ex Auditis et Visis* [Heaven and Its Wonders and Hell: Drawn from Things Heard and Seen]. London: 1758.

INTERCOURSE BETWEEN THE SOUL AND BODY
Modern Title: *Soul-Body Interaction*
Original Title: *De Commercio Animae et Corporis, Quod Creditur Fieri vel per Influxum Physicum, vel per Influxum Spiritualem, vel per Harmoniam Praestabilitam* [Soul-Body Interaction, Believed to Occur either by a Physical Inflow, or by a Spiritual Inflow, or by a Preestablished Harmony]. London: 1769.

THE LAST JUDGMENT
Modern Title: *Last Judgment*
Original Title: *De Ultimo Judicio, et de Babylonia Destructa: Ita Quod Omnia, Quae in Apocalypsi Praedicta Sunt, Hodie Impleta Sunt: Ex Auditis et Visis* [The Last Judgment and Babylon Destroyed, Showing That at This Day All the Predictions of the Book of Revelation Have Been Fulfilled: Drawn from Things Heard and Seen]. London: 1758.

NEW JERUSALEM AND ITS HEAVENLY DOCTRINE
Modern Title: *New Jerusalem*
Original Title: *De Nova Hierosolyma et Ejus Doctrina Coelesti: Ex Auditis e Coelo: Quibus Praemittitur Aliquid de Novo Coelo et Nova Terra* [The New Jerusalem and Its Heavenly Teaching: Drawn from Things Heard from Heaven: Preceded by a Discussion of the New Heaven and the New Earth]. London: 1758.

SPIRITUAL DIARY
Modern title: *Spiritual Experiences*
Original title: *Experientiae Spirituales* [Spiritual Experiences]. London: 1844 (published posthumously).

TRUE CHRISTIAN RELIGION
Modern Title: *True Christianity*
Original Title: *Vera Christiana Religio, Continens Universam Theologiam Novae Ecclesiae a Domino apud Danielem Cap. VII:13–14, et in Apocalypsi Cap. XXI:1, 2 Praedictae* [True Christianity: Containing a

Comprehensive Theology of the New Church That Was Predicted by the Lord in Daniel 7:13–14 and Revelation 21:1, 2]. Amsterdam: 1771.

THE WHITE HORSE
Modern Title: *White Horse*
Original title: *De Equo Albo, de Quo in Apocalypsi, Cap. XIX: Et Dein de Verbo et Ejus Sensu Spirituali seu Interno, ex Arcanis Coelestibus* [The White Horse in Revelation Chapter 19, and the Word and Its Spiritual or Inner Sense (from Secrets of Heaven)]. London: 1758.

INDEX

Bolded page numbers refer to the main entry on that topic.